THE OTHER SAT

Systematic Adolescent Theology

FOURTH EDITION

James Gamble, Ph.D.

ISBN: 061555735X
ISBN-13: 978-0615557359

DEDICATION

This book is dedicated to my beautiful wife, Lucinda, and our two wonderful 'kids': JJ & Marcy.

CONTENTS

ACKNOWLEDGMENTS

Thanks to God who gives us the victory through our Lord, Jesus Christ.

Thanks to my beautiful wife, Lucinda and my awesome kids JJ and Marcy whom have all been pillars of support and inspiration.

Thanks to the rest of my family and friends who have been entirely encouraging and so supportive.

Thanks to the pastors and church leaders whom God has used to shape and strengthen my walk in Christ.

Thanks to the Christian educators who have dedicated a portion of their lives to educate so many in Biblical truth.

Thanks to my niece, Kenyetta Hall, for the remarkable artwork.

Thanks to those who assisted in editing various portions of this work:
Mrs. Mary E. Knight (Alpha & Omega Proofreading Service, LLP)
Dr. Doris Rash-Konneh (The Writing Doctor)
Dr. Corena Miller (Computer Services + eLearning)
Mrs. Kathy King-Avery.

FOREWORD

Every so often in life you meet someone who you genuinely like right off the bat. For me, James Gamble is just such a person. James and I first met in the context of a student-professor relationship several years ago -- I was the professor and James was the student. I have always believed that students have just as much to teach professors as professors do students -- that axiom has proven to be true with James. You see, James is the epitome of a disciple because he is "a learner" in every sense of the word. Learners love to fellowship with one another, they love to bounce ideas off one another, they love to share books they have read, and they love to have things they have written critiqued by those whom they respect as a fellow-learner. Learners love spending time with other learners because they are kindred spirits. Learners love to learn and they love to help others learn.

James has written a book titled *The Other SAT*. The subtitle "Systematic Adolescent Theology" is an accurate description of the

1

contents of the book. Simply put, James has a burden that the young people of this world truly know God in all His awesome majesty. He is aware that many young adults in contemporary culture are being "destroyed for lack of knowledge" (Hosea 4:6). Furthermore, James knows that there is no greater pursuit in life than the knowledge of God (John 17:3). Toward that end James has written about knowing God and today's young Christian men and women are at the forefront of this endeavor.

The Other SAT is written to the adolescent but the information is not "dumbed down" so as to prove insulting to a contemporary young man or woman. In seven well-written chapters, James develops the overall theme of the knowledge of God:

- What is the Other SAT?

- Obtaining Knowledge of God

- Sharing the Knowledge of God

- Proving the Knowledge of God

- Reproving the Knowledge of Man

- Exposing the Knowledge of Man

- Applying the Knowledge of God

James demonstrates that rare ability to communicate large quantities of Biblical information in a creative and palatable manner. In fact, the didactic teaching material in this text is like a mini seminary education between two covers! My prayer is that it will be read widely and used to transform the lives of thousands of young men and women.

Dr. Ron Cobb –Chair, Department of Biblical Counseling

Luther Rice University

Lithonia (Atlanta), Georgia

INTRODUCTION

A guy by the name of Tom Bisset conducted 18 months of interviews and a great deal of study on the subject of Christian youth who, as he puts it, walk away from their Christian faith. In his book, *Why Christian Kids Leave the Faith*, he lists four reasons he discovered as to why Christian kids 'leave the faith'. Out of all the reasons he lists, the one that sticks out in my mind is: "they have troubling, unanswered questions about their faith."[1]

Apparently, instead of a foundational knowledge of God and a relationship with God based on that knowledge those kids only had information about God and an acquaintance with Him. That lack of knowledge has left several unanswered questions. They never really established themselves in the Christian faith. So, it's not that they left a faith in God through Jesus Christ, which they had established for themselves. They simply stopped pursuing the idea of establishing a faith in God. That makes more sense to me, but we will make use of Bisset's expression that they 'left the faith'. My goal is not to argue against Mr. Bisset. I am grateful for his research and am not at variance (I don't disagree) with the results produced by it. It doesn't matter whether we view their exodus as having left the faith or having never established their place in the faith. Either way, we realize a very grave situation and Bisset exposes it very well. He concludes, "Unwilling to 'just believe,' they opt for 'intellectual honesty.' To do this they believe they must leave their childhood faith behind in order to find real answers in the real world."[2]

Let me try and explain the magnitude of Bisset's concluding statement. First, "intellectual honesty" is more than just 'not cheating on tests and homework' and 'not plagiarizing (copying) someone else's work'. Intellectual honesty implies that anything not physically seeable is not fully believable and is therefore debatable. It is considered an "idea," because general philosophy holds that one cannot obtain complete intellectual honesty. Intellectual honesty is a cute way to say all things are debatable. The purpose for the debate is to make sure argument has been allowed in favor of and against a statement so that we can fully determine whether the statement is true or false. So, intellectual honesty encourages us to make sure every theory and every belief (perhaps even every statement) we make has a physical, seeable fact in front of it.

Intellectual honesty is an excellent tool for academia in that it acts as a check valve for educated folks–especially within institutions of higher learning—who wish to push their unproven theories and assumptions onto the unlearned or uninformed. In the world of academia, knowledge is considered somewhat sacred. So, they who value truth require those who present truths to others do so with purity and honesty. Those involved with the academic system know there is a certain level of anxiety or eagerness to learn and even a bit of intimidation with not knowing that causes some learners to not stop and verify what they are being told by their educators. So, with intellectual honesty in place, if what an educator is saying doesn't meet academia's criteria of intellectual honesty (if it's not a proven fact), then it gets checked at the valve and is sent back in the direction from which it came. That's when the check valve works properly. Intellectual honesty is an excellent tool for academia—when it is adhered to. There have been cases where some in academia have not been true to the principle of intellectual honesty as we'll discuss later.

The only problem with intellectual honesty outside of academic purposes is it leaves no room for faith. Being intellectually honest means (again) everything is debatable. Remember, philosophy holds that one cannot totally achieve intellectual honesty. So, in the philosophical world there is always room for debate. Even if there is clear and physical evidence of a thing, according to intellectual honesty, one can still debate it. To me this defies logic—you know—plain old common sense.

There are clearly some things in nature or in the physical realm that are not debatable. If we're looking at a green car and you say it's red, you've created a reason for debate, but the fact that the car is green is really not debatable. We can go back and forth all day long with arguments on why we see the car differently, but that won't change the color of the car. The color of the car is not debatable. Likewise, there are clearly some things that we cannot debate in the Spiritual realm. People can create a reason for debate, but that doesn't change the facts found in the Bible. Biblical facts are not debatable.

So then, we can measure any non-factual 'theories' or 'beliefs' outside of the Bible against Biblical truths and see if they have the possibility of being true. If they go against Biblical facts, then we, as Christians, should not entertain those theories or beliefs as truths. If that isn't enough for you, however, you can still evaluate them within their own system of 'intellectual honesty' and then see whether or not they are truths. We will evaluate a few, just for the sake of 'debate'–pun intended.

We as a people of faith don't need to "opt for intellectual honesty" in cases where all it does is debate Biblical facts or dissuade faith. We should gather all the knowledge we can outside of Biblical knowledge for whatever profession we expect to enter into. However, we don't have to exclude our faith in our knowledge-gathering efforts. Our fact-collection does not have to compete with our faith. We can maintain our faith in Biblical facts and still accumulate a wealth of knowledge beyond that. If we stay with the facts found in the Bible, we are not being dishonest to our intellect.

Those who argue that intellectual honesty needs to be absent of faith, do so because they believe faith will hinder the academic process. They claim we who are faithful to God through Jesus Christ will leave out fact if it interferes with our faith. Consequently, those intellectually-inclined folks feel the same about people of other faiths/religions. So, don't think we're special in that regard. Faith in God does not hinder the academic process. In fact, faith in God *is* an academic process. Our faith is not obtained through unintelligible ways (we don't just believe regardless of what the facts are). God has proven Himself over and over. Because we know (through our own experiences as well as others') God has always proven Himself, we believe if anything else comes along and tries to disprove Him, He will prove Himself again. That's the essence of our faith. God has proven Himself. Why believe something else?

If scientists have proven the chemical makeup of water is hydrogen and oxygen, why go looking to see if there is a third element in there? Each time you try to prove there is more in pure water than hydrogen and oxygen, you're going to fail. The reason you will fail is because it has already been proven: hydrogen + oxygen = water (mixed in the proper proportions, of course).

Now, listen to the trailing part of Bisset's statement, again: "…they believe they must leave their childhood faith behind." Since intellectual honesty (unchecked) leaves no room for faith, if a person chooses to go all out with this thing, then they feel they must leave their faith behind. I suppose this is where we get the old saying, "I have to go find myself." What a scary thought. What happens if somebody finds themself somewhere they don't want to be? What do they do while they try to get to where they need to be–especially without faith?

Now, before I get all the educators on a witch hunt (with me as the witch), let me clarify some things. We should be honest with our intellect. Intellectual honesty is not an evil within itself. Just like a loaded gun is not an evil within itself. In both cases, someone has to misuse the thing for it to cause harm. Intellectual honesty just aims to force people to get their facts together before they present information to others they claim as truths.

Having the facts before making a statement should be everyone's objective. And we should always speak up when someone makes an incorrect statement. The same holds true in any environment in which we find ourselves (school, church, work, anywhere). That's how we mature in the learning process. That's how we help others mature in this process. Learning is the practice of gaining the facts. The world of academia is essential in propagating facts. But again, facts do not have to compete with faith. In fact (no pun intended), if your faith is properly placed then every fact you stumble upon will just increase your faith. It's the non-facts that throw people for a loop.

We Christians should never consider leaving our faith in search of facts. We never have to leave our faith behind to find ourselves. That's really scary. We know who we are because of our faith–Children of the

King! That's a fact! Whoa, I almost broke out into a sermon, there. Let me get back to our intellectual discussion.

The reason I keep saying finding yourself is scary is because reading Bisset's book is not the first time I encountered the notion that some young people leave the faith because of new found knowledge especially in their college years. When I was fifteen years old, a young adult family member (in college at the time) introduced me to Jesus Christ. Oh, I had been in church for years and had heard over and over about this Guy named Jesus; but this family member brought me to an understanding of who Jesus really is to us Christians. That person showed me His place in God's plan of salvation (which I had not seen before). Then, they made sure I understood what I needed to do to obtain that salvation. The person then prayed with me and I accepted Jesus Christ, the Savior.

Years later, the same person stated they didn't believe in God, but rather thought the universe is god. Can you imagine how many times the question went through my mind: "What happened to make this person leave the faith they introduced me to? How is that possible?" I asked them and they told me they never really believed in Jesus Christ. So, it was not that they left the faith. They never were established in the faith. They simply stopped pursuing it.

That person explained to me their only means of paying for college at that time was to accept a theological scholarship at a popular nearby university. The person accepted the scholarship and majored in theology, but minored in the area of study in which they were truly interested. Their encounter with me to share God's plan of salvation was just a project for a grade. Well, it was just a grade for them, but for me, it really was in God's plan.

I now see this person had not really developed their own faith in God. Their misuse (or maybe misunderstanding) of "intellectual honesty" left them no desire in building faith. So they chose not to pursue a relationship with God through Christ any further or in Bisset's words, they left the faith.

When I saw the title of Bisset's book, I was crushed with the idea of folks presumably leaving the faith. I say presumably (seemingly), because [again] it's apparent those folks have not yet developed a faith. Still, how could they walk away from something that had more substance than anything else they will ever encounter? How could they leave this quest for something that, by its own confession, can never find all the answers? Remember, philosophy admits we cannot attain true intellectual honesty. The questions and debates just go on and on and on. How can someone choose that over faith in God? I pondered that heavily at one time. I don't anymore. Now, I don't worry myself with if and why they will leave the faith. I'm more concerned with getting them to stay with it until they completely develop it.

Thus, the intent of this book is to propose another angle to Tom Bisset's question. Rather than try and determine why Christian kids leave the faith, it attempts to answer the question, "How can we make

Christian kids never want to leave the faith?" Keep in mind leaving the faith, in this case, means they chose to not pursue a relationship with God, even after they have heard of Him. I know I've emphasized it several times, but I need to make sure that part is understood.

Evidence gained through research, observation and survey proves we can reduce the 'dropout-rate' of young Christians pursuing to establish their faith in God. Evidence also shows we can increase the enlistment impact young Christians will have on others in persuading them to consider pursuit of a faith in God through Jesus Christ. I am convinced we can move from worrying if our kids will leave their pursuit of a relationship with God to knowing they will accomplish it. I am convinced first by the Word of God (cf. Proverbs 22:6, Titus 1:9, and 1 Peter 3:15) and secondly by observation (scientific proof–if we can borrow the term). You can read those referenced Bible verses at your leisure and get Biblical reassurance there. Let me share the observable proof side of this.

After I sort of took in what Mr. Bisset had proclaimed about why Christian kids leave the faith, I decided to try and determine if this was the case with any of our youth. I asked myself, "Are our youth losing their desire to pursue a relationship with God?" We were having some issues with reaching our young people at church. Our Youth Ministry was struggling a little bit. For some reason they didn't understand us grown folks and we apparently didn't understand them. You know the story: generational gaps and changing culture and the like.

The youth ministry was in trouble because of that. Somehow we needed to get past the generational indifferences and figure out what was really going on. I asked for permission to develop and issue an anonymously submitted survey to the youth to get an understanding of what they felt was wrong. The Youth Council agreed this might be a good way to gauge what was wrong and determine how to best correct it. They decided the ages should be the youth ages 13-18 and young adults ages 19-40.

The survey proved Bisset's first reason accurate. The youth felt the curriculum was not enough to keep their interest or to help them grow in their faith. This, according to Bisset's research, left "troubling, unanswered questions about their faith." The survey also proved Bisset's fourth reason for why kids drop out was accurate. They were tired of just following along and wanted to have much more involvement in establishing their own faith. According to Bisset's research, "They never personally owned their faith." The survey revealed other issues as well, but these two aligned with what Bisset's extensive research had shown and what could be currently seen, so they caught my attention the most. I realized more than ever that we needed to do something to help those teens establish their faith in God. If we didn't, they were in perfect position to be one of Bisset's statistics.

After reviewing the results of the surveys, my next questions were: How do we get our young people to establish their faith in God? How do we get them to build a meaningful relationship with Him? How do we get them to attune their personal lives to the Word of God? How do we get them to want to not just talk about God, but remember God long after Sunday school and Bible Study is over? How do we get them to want to move that remembrance of God to more than just knowledge, but an actual relationship with Him through His Son? How do we get them to do it now, in the days of their youth?

If we wait until they are older and 'settled' we will forfeit the initial opportunity to set the foundation for what they know and believe. It allows someone else to set the course for what they will understand and believe about the world around them. They will place their faith in something other than God. Now, if we Christian educators will not take the lead, secular academia will gladly step in and take the position of being the one to set the course for what our youth understand and believe about the world around them.

I know there are many folks out there in the secular education field who are Christians and would never mislead one of our precious youth. There are also others who are not Christians who mean *all* students well and therefore would not purposely mislead them. I can't state this enough: I'm not trying to paint an evil picture of secular education. There is certainly a need in the lives of Christian youth for the fundamental education obtained in the secular school system. There is a much greater need, however, for a Biblical education in their crucial developing years. Knowledge of God is imperative (crucial) if youth are to maintain their Christian faith once they step outside of the all-Christian environment.

It is not bashing the school system to say they are not in support of our kids' development of Christian faith. This is simply stating a fact. We know of the court rulings that disallow mentioning of God or even expression of religion in schools. John W. Whitehead, president of The Rutherford Institute, states in a news article for the Associated Press, "We've become so politically correct in terms of how we deal with religion that it's being pretty severely limited in schools right now, and individuals suffer."

To be honest with you, I prefer "religion" not be taught in public schools. If it were, then our kids would be forced to be subjected to anybody's religion. This is not about religion; however, this is about faith. If my kid already has a faith, my kid should be able to maintain that faith without it being an offense to someone else. A teacher should be able to maintain the same faith—or any other faith for that matter—without offending anyone. Having faith just means believing in something. No one should be offended by another person's beliefs. Beliefs are not offensive. It's the accompanying actions of some beliefs that are offensive.

Public schools are obviously not the ones who will increase our Christian kids' faith. In fact, if we analyze all of the data we have, we see that schools are taking steps, which can cause a severe decrease of our kids' faith. It doesn't matter if this is intentional or not. In that respect, Mr. Whitehead is absolutely correct in saying "…individuals suffer." Calling them individuals sounds too impersonal, though. Those individuals are our kids.

This book purposes to educate youth in the Christian faith, so they will develop and maintain a meaningful love and respect for God through Jesus Christ. My goal is to simplify some of the terms, concepts and theories theologians have drawn from Biblical truth. I do not intend to address every aspect of theology (that might take an entire library of books—not to mention *I* can't do it anyway). My objective is to try and reduce the complexity of the basic theology of Christianity. The basic theology presented in the Bible is God wants to restore a meaningful relationship with humankind; and He has made provisions for doing so.

This book also serves as a small accumulation of information concerning a few academic theories and beliefs that badly contradict Bible truth. Along with the contradictions are facts that prove those theories and beliefs make false claims at being truth. In other words, it shows where those theories and beliefs have not held true to their own principles of "intellectual honesty". In some cases, we will see they have been intellectually dishonest. The theories and beliefs selected as the topics of discussion for this book are those that appear to be the most popular in secular education. For that reason, they are the most probable to be accepted as fact by our young people.

Explanation will be given for any terms (theological or otherwise) I feel some young people may not be familiar with. There will be a lot of parentheses and restatements. I have also included a glossary at the end of the book to serve as a help for unfamiliar words and terms. I am doing this because I feel most adolescents will not stop to grab a dictionary or thesaurus for words they do not understand. I don't believe they will stop and re-read something they did not get the first time. Well, maybe you did as a young person, but I didn't. I would just keep reading, hoping to 'understand it by and by'.

Hopefully, including the unfamiliar terms with the common words and terms and restating things differently will help expand the understanding and vocabulary of our young readers. That way when they mature enough for the 'deeper things' in theology, they will not be apprehensive, but will already have been introduced to them. This approach is taught often in the Bible (cf. 1 Corinthians 3:1-2, Hebrews 5:12-14, 1 Peter 2:2), so we should feel very safe with using this systematic approach.

Please join me in my enthusiasm to train our Christian youth up in the way they should go, so they won't be persuaded to go a different route later. Hopefully you will agree with the Biblical model that a sound doctrine will prevent our youth from straying and cause them to be a vessel for presenting Christ to others. The more information youth have to respond against non-truth, the more eager they will be to respond with the truth. The whole idea is to place as much effort in this SAT (Systematic Adolescent Theology), as some of us have placed in the original SAT (Scholastic Aptitude Test). We want to prepare our young people for the next crucial phase in their lives whether it is college, military, or the workforce. Our kids are going to see and hear a lot of new things in their young adult years. Some of those things will test their faith. If we give them something to build their faith on, our kids will mature in their relationship with Jesus Christ and no one will be able to entice them to walk away from that relationship.

1 WHAT IS THE OTHER SAT?

If you'll arm yourself with the knowledge of God, you can maintain your faith through anything. (Rf. Proverbs 22:6)

The Other SAT

I'm not trying to trick anybody in borrowing the popular SAT acronym. I just thought this would catch the attention of you young folks preparing for or already attending college, as well as old folks trying to help you get there. Even those who aren't going to college would probably want to know why somebody's coming out with another SAT; as if one wasn't enough! I feel sure if you see a book on the shelf about the "Other SAT," you'll take a second look. You'll want to see what you missed on the first go-round. You will probably want to see if there really is more help for college-bound students. Well, there is, but it's nothing like the first SAT. I wanted to capture the essence of the importance for preparing for college, but in a totally different light. I just threw in the look-alike cover for cheap advertisement.

College years, as we know, are very instrumental in shaping a young adult's view of the world. New students are presented with lots of fresh material, which they will have to digest according to their current worldview (their understanding of how the world works). Once they get a good dose of information shaped and formulated by other worldviews, they must then decide if their own worldview should change or if it should or can remain the same. As a Christian student you are no exception. You will have to gather all that info, process it and decide if you will use it for the rest of your life or check it at the door when you leave the classroom.

Since most worldviews presented in academia are not Christian worldviews, you may face questions that will eat away at your Christian faith. As a young Christian, your faith can really be shaken up by some of the information you'll encounter as you leave the nest of safety your Christian parents or guardians have provided you for so long. But, your faith will be shaken up only if it is undeveloped–only if you don't already have a good grounding in your Christian faith.

Systematic

With that said, a definition of this other SAT (Systematic Adolescent Theology) is in order. There may be some readers who have reservations with the concept. No doubt, some of you (or your parents or mentors) are thinking, "Here we go, again–another new wave of thinking. Look out!" Well, this is definitely *not* a new concept. In fact, it's just a combination of old ones; neatly packaged.

Systematic (as we use it here) means reduced complexity, streamlined, methodical steps taken to come to the concluded facts found in study. All that means is taking a subject and learning just the core elements of it. It does not take away from the principle of diligent study in determining the facts; as some might fear. It just presents the facts in smaller (maybe even fewer), more manageable pieces. A systematic approach can get you grounded in the truth while allowing for other components to be added later. The idea here is to get young folks 'grounded in truth' before sending them off to 'soar with eagles'.

We still want you to fly; we just want you to be headed on the right course when you take off.

Adolescent

Adolescent, as many are probably aware, refers to someone who is in the phase of life that hovers between childhood and adulthood. Most of us adults have just determined it to be a grey area. At what point do you really grow up? When do you even begin to? We've almost given up on figuring that one out. We'll just let you tell us when you think you're there.

Yeah, right–don't expect many adults to take that approach to getting you through adolescence. That's just my good-humored way of explaining this tough stage in your lives. To understand exactly what an adolescent is, however, let's check with the experts. *The Journal of Adolescent Research* considers adolescence to be ages ten to eighteen. The journal is edited by Jeffrey Jensen Arnett, Ph.D., Chair of the Special Interest Group on Emerging Adulthood Sponsored by the Society for Research on Adolescence. Did you get all of that guy's title? Wow. That's a bit much.

Most of my experiences with youth have been with the ten to eighteen age group. I can say from those experiences that not all of you go from childhood to adulthood in the same manner or during the same timeframe. Observation has proven some are forced to deal with adult-like situations long before they become of age and tend to act mature earlier than we think they ought. Others never have to make decisions or think things out for themselves and take much longer than expected to mature. The experts may have a broader scope of data than I have, though, so this book will use the age ranges Dr. Arnett suggests: ten to eighteen.

Theology

Finally, theology simply means the study of God. It is what you can *and do* know about God. There are a lot of long, complicated definitions available for the term (the *Merriam-Webster's Desk Dictionary* alone has four). Long and complicated is not necessary. This one will suffice (work just fine) for us. The idea here is to keep it simple. The simplest definition of theology (based on Merriam-Webster, a few authors of theology textbooks, and a few professors I've had in the past is–the study of God. By the way, unless otherwise specified, the *Merriam-Webster's Desk Dictionary* (Merriam-Webster) will be used for all English word definitions in this book outside of the glossary. The glossary may contain simplified definitions aimed at enhancing your understanding.

Now, we old folks like to have reusable labels for the topics we study. That's why most preachers give you a title for their sermons. That's why your classes have a course title on your syllabi. It helps you to associate the entire message or course of study with a general objective when you include a catchy title. Our objective here is to systematically provide knowledge of God for young folks to build and share their faith. So let's call it Systematic Adolescent Theology–pretty catchy, huh? Okay, maybe not, but it works. And just for the record, this book defines Systematic Adolescent Theology as the non-complex, methodical steps one can take to prepare youth and young adults with what one has studied and knows about God and how they might share it with others.

Apologetics

I suppose this is a good place to define apologetics, too, since we will be using the apologetic process to help you to learn and share a few things about God. Apologetic refers to how Christians present what they know about God to non-Christians (as well as refute [prove false] wrong information about God that non-Christians present to others). Apologetics (as it is used in this book and in accordance with 1 Peter 3:15) offer answers to questions for why we believe what we believe–as opposed to giving an excuse or an apology for it. We'll talk more about that later.

Origin of the Concept: The Original SAT

It is amazing the reaction you get when you mention or display the infamous acronym, SAT to teenage students getting ready for college. Boy! They get excited about those three letters. Well, most kids get excited. Some don't want to hear it. Some are petrified at the mere thought of SAT. Either way, the SAT acronym (an abbreviation of a set of words using only the first letter of each word) really gets young folks to respond.

Kids begin to talk about fears of taking the exams or the achievement of having done so and having passed it. They start talking about retakes and getting a better score. They want to get the best score they possibly can before time to submit those scores to colleges along with their application packets.

My wife and I have two young people in college (at the time of writing this), so we are very familiar with how hyped folks get about this SAT thing. Some parents really go to great lengths to prepare their kids for the SAT. Not only do parents want to ensure their kids do well on the SAT, but they also want to make sure they have prepared their kids in other areas. They just want their children to make it at the next level of their precious, youthful lives. As I recall the relentless enthusiasm during our kids' final high school years, I remember the orchestrated madness (controlled chaos) displayed in us and other parents, as well as the teachers and high school staff.

The coaches were going through one more round of educating their athletes on the importance of self-discipline in their physical training and eating habits. They were double-checking to make sure highlights of their best game performances had made it to college coaches in ample (enough) time for review. Counselors were double-checking transcripts and volunteer hours to make sure the kids had completed the hours of education and community service required for graduation. Teachers were giving students pointers on how to survive the first year of college life. They were encouraging them to maintain good study habits and to choose their friends wisely. Military JROTC officers were motivating their young cadets for an abrupt (quick; rough) transition into military life at the academy or training camp. Parents were sharing priceless information with one another on practice and preparation steps for helping their kids to obtain the best SAT scores, get into the best schools, and find the best scholarships. They all wanted to present opportunities to those kids and wanted those kids to take full advantage of them.

You probably remember or are currently experiencing some of it. If not yet, it's coming. When it comes, there will be an assortment of activities going on around you to make sure you are prepared to continue in your course of study or become whatever in life you desire to be.

Parents, teachers, counselors, and coaches will do all they can to prepare you. They know from experience that if you prepare for an event (life in this case), you will be more apt (able) to make it through the event as you intend. Of course, it does not guarantee success at all of life's endeavors, but it does increase your possibilities. It places the potential there, which just needs to be coupled (combined/joined) with your aspiration (desire). If you desire to do well and have the training it takes to do well, eventually you will do well.

That's the reason for this other SAT (Systematic Adolescent Theology). It aims to place the same enthusiasm into getting you ready from a Christian faith perspective to make it through the next phase in your precious life. Your faith is almost certain to be challenged at some point in the young adult phase of your life. If you take the necessary steps to arm yourself with the knowledge of God, you can maintain your faith through those challenging moments.

Biblical Principle

The message in Proverbs 22:6 is basically that. It reads, "Train up a child in the way he should go, even when he is old he will not depart from it." Unless you see another version of the Bible in parenthesis after a verse, the New American Standard Bible (NASB)[1] will be used throughout this book for Scripture references. The message in the passage (section) of Scripture found in Proverbs 22:6 is centered on three key words: train, old, and depart. Well, let's start by clarifying the "he" in that passage of Scripture. Often when the Scriptures read "he" or "man" it refers to the human race. So the "he" in Proverbs 22:6 refers to both male and female. We don't have to waste time defining train—you know what it means to train someone. To fully understand this passage, though, the other two key words ("old" and "depart") need to be viewed from the Hebrew context in which they were written.

We'll be using *The Brown-Driver-Briggs Hebrew and English Lexicon*[2] for our Hebrew translations throughout the book—again unless the notes state otherwise. The Old Testament was originally written in the Hebrew language. So, to get a good understanding of what it is saying; we may have to look up the Hebrew meaning of words from time to time.

The way words are used sometimes change with the changing of culture. The root meaning never changes, but the word's understanding in one cultural setting may be different than that of another. Take for instance the word geek. When computers first began to become popular, the term computer geek was considered very derogatory (insulting). Now the term (at least among those in the business world) is very respectable. In fact, the Geek Squad (a company owned by Best Buy) seems widely used for installation and repair of technical merchandise. Their iconic (highly recognizable) police car-looking Volkswagen Beetles can be seen all around the U.S. Their employees are proud to be called geeks now; however, a few years ago they would have frowned on such. So, word values change as cultures change, even though the root meaning remains the same.

The original Hebrew word used in Proverbs 22:6 for old is *zaqen* which means to become old or to show age. To become old or to show age in both the culture at that time in Bible history and our modern western culture means the same thing; and that is "to mature." To mature in understanding something means to finally get it.

The original Hebrew word used for depart in Proverbs 22:6 is *cuwr* (pronounced soor) which means to "be taken away." That's a bit different than what we understand depart to mean. We think of departing as leaving on our own. The ancient Hebrews saw it as being pulled or drawn away.

So, we can read this Scripture passage to say: If we train our children in the Word of God in a way that they get it, then once they get it; they cannot be drawn away from it. The youth Bisset discussed in his book either had not been trained up in Biblical truth or they were not maturing in their understanding of this truth (they didn't get it). Because they did not get it, their faith was being riddled with (full of) doubt and eventually (as Bisset presents) they stopped pursuing maturity of their faith. They were drawn away from a desire to know God better. That's the message of the text found in Proverbs 22:6.

Jesus gave the same message in a parable (life depicting story) He told to His disciples. It is recorded in Mark 4:1-20, Matthew 13:1-23, and Luke 8:1-15. Check it out some time. The message Jesus gives is many hear the Word of God, but fail to grow into an understanding of it. Jesus says in Mark 4:20, "…while seeing, they may see and not perceive (comprehend), and while hearing, they may hear and not understand…" If they don't understand God, then their faith cannot mature before they are drawn away.

Life experiences prove the maturation process (becoming older and/or wiser) does not generally happen without a few bumps and bruises. However, once a person matures in something (once they get a grasp of what they are being trained on), they have it for good. This is evident in the old adage (saying): "Get a good education. That is something no one can take from you." If you're like me you're thinking what I was thinking back in my high school days: "I've had enough of school. After high school, I'm done!" Trust me, many who opted out of college back in their day wish they would have gone or stayed. In fact, many (including myself) wind up going back to school and juggling family responsibilities, a career, and even ministry while trying to obtain a college degree. Do yourself a favor; stay in school. Oh, and don't do drugs.

Many adults can attest to (tell about) having had their share of bumps and bruises in their life-learning experiences. Proverbs 22:6 does not guarantee a young person who has been trained up "in the discipline and instruction of the Lord" (as Ephesians 6:4 puts it) will not make a few learning-about-life mistakes from time to time. It means proper training will give you a foundational understanding of God's Word (which is required to know Him). Once you accept Christ and mature in your knowledge of God, that foundation cannot be taken away.

Principles from Study, Training, and Experience

Bisset's conclusion becomes very realistic when we consider the reasons young people seem to stop pursuing a relationship with God once they go off to college or leave their homes as young adults. Their undeveloped faith gets shaken (they are persuaded to doubt what little they know), because they do not have a good foundational knowledge of why they believe what they believe. When faith is shaken, folks begin to entertain discussions that go against what they know and believe. It doesn't matter if those discussions are crammed with non-facts. If you're not well-grounded, it introduces doubt, because you can't discern fact from non-fact. It was an element of doubt that caused Eve (and subsequently, Adam) to be separated from God by sin.

After sitting through a few seminary courses centered on theology and apologetics, I realized how important it is for kids (anyone for that matter) to be prepared to respond to questions about their faith. I found there is so much not covered by parents and teachers in youth Sunday school and Bible study that needs to be covered. We parents and teachers seem to place a whole lot of emphasis on other areas of your lives (education, finances, health, relationships), but almost totally neglect the area of Spirituality (helping you to know God in a personal way through Jesus Christ). There were so many questions in those seminary courses answered for me that I thought might never be answered. Many misconceptions (misunderstandings) were corrected as well.

I know. Not everyone needs to or wants to go to a Bible college or seminary. I certainly would encourage it, but we know people can learn as much as they need to know to have a healthy, meaningful relationship with Jesus Christ from good pastors and Christian educators in the church–along with studying on your own. Whichever of these routes we choose in obtaining knowledge of God is fine. We just need to choose one. Otherwise, we will never mature in our relationship with Him.

Purpose of SAT: Biblical Incentive for Apologetics

We discussed before that theology is the study of God. That means theology answers questions about God for people. We must take time to study the Word of God if we are to get answers to our questions about God. We must study also to answer questions others have about God. Once we study, the questions *we* have concerning God become fewer; then we are better equipped to answer questions others ask us about Him. Apologetics, as stated earlier, are how Christians present those answers to non-Christians (as well as refute [prove false] wrong information non-Christians present to us).

I've spoken with some who are very well-grounded in the Gospel message of our Lord and Savior Jesus Christ who oppose (disagree with) the idea of apologetics. So, I feel a need to expound on the subject (talk about it). Some folks I've talked with have expressed the idea that apologetics is just apologizing for being a Christian. By their own admission, they see no need to explain God to folks from an angle that debates points or facts. They feel the right approach is to express who God is and let the other person be either convinced or convicted based on their faith. They feel it will be the person's faith that moves them into a relationship with God in Christ.

Their point is very valid and very scripturally sound when it comes to faith. Faith is the basic element in knowing and loving God. This is the understanding that is exemplified (made clear) in Hebrews 11:6– "But without faith it is impossible to please him: for he that cometh to

God must believe that he is, and that he is a rewarder of them that diligently seek him." However, Romans 10:17 illustrates that faith in God comes by hearing the Word of God. The Greek word for hearing in this passage of Scripture is akoe (pronounced ak-o-ay'), which means oral instruction. Oral instruction is not just for casual listening. It is given with the purpose of helping someone to understand something. So, we must understand the Word of God, before we can build a faith in it. And we must help others understand it, if they are to believe as we. That's the intent of apologetics.

Again, we will occasionally go to the original words of the Bible text to better understand the message. The New Testament was originally written in Greek. So, we'll be using *A Manual Greek Lexicon of the New Testament*[3] for our Greek translations throughout this book—unless the notes state otherwise.

You're starting to get the hang of this notation thing by now, right? We have to give credit to those folks who put so much hard work into providing us with help in our studies. So, every time we use their information in our papers, books, etc. we give them credit by noting where we got the information. If you've written term papers, you already know that.

You can't have faith in something you have no knowledge of. So, someone who knows God has to instruct others on who God is. Instruction is given to make known what is unknown, to answer questions, and even to remove doubts. That is exactly what apologetics does. If people do not have knowledge of the love of God and the power of God, then what is there to generate their faith in God? They can know there *is* a God without our mention of Him. Evidence of God is seen in nature (see Romans 1:20), but to have faith in Him, one must hear about (or learn of) Him. Apologetics allows the non-Christian to hear and know the Christian's story of why he or she believes what they believe.

This book does not attempt to minimize the realism and necessity of faith. In fact, its function is to increase faith. As you continue, you will clearly see that promoting faith in God and the Savior, Jesus Christ, is the sole purpose for the apologetic process. It takes a great deal of faith to speak against false doctrine and ungodly worldviews held by others while speaking in support of Biblical truth. It takes a great deal of faith to give an answer to hard questions aimed at insulting Christian doctrine. Through faith we know any information that contradicts Biblical truth will prove itself false. Through faith we as Christians know any philosophy that contradicts Biblical truth will find itself vain. Through faith we know any worldview that contradicts Biblical truth will prove itself lacking and empty and will eventually implode (destroy itself or prove itself wrong).

Unwillingness to defend how we Christians came about our faith does not benefit those folks who have no faith or those who have their faith placed in the wrong belief systems. Unwillingness to defend our faith leaves others with the idea that we Christians do not have an answer for why we believe what we believe. They think we just believe.

We must share our faith in a way that causes others to objectively (without bias or prejudice) consider our view so they will have an opportunity to believe as we believe, thus establishing their own Christian faith. Non-Christians will need facts upon which to establish their faith. Well, we Christians have the facts, so why not share them?

Apologetics never attempts to make us apologize for being a Christian. As stated before, the apologetic process offers answers to questions for why Christians believe what they believe. The reason for being prepared to defend our faith is it helps us maintain this faith, and it proves accusations against our faith to be false. Most importantly, it allows us to share our faith with others.

By the way, apologetics is not an attempt to ridicule those with little or no knowledge of God. We don't learn the Bible just so we can impress or embarrass others with what we know about God. The entire apologetic process is done in such a way that proves one's own faith, without any attempt to offend another's faith. It begins with a pureness in the message along with meekness in the attitude and ends the same way. This offers the non-Christian the opportunity to objectively evaluate (study with an open mind) this faith of ours against their own (or lack thereof) and make a choice as to which is beneficial to them. The entire passage in 1 Peter 3:15 reads as this:

but sanctify Christ as Lord in your hearts, always being ready to make a defense to everyone who asks you to give an account for the hope that is in you, yet with gentleness and reverence;

I'm not trying to gear you up for an intellectual fight in the classroom. We don't need any unruly radicals for Christ. Radicals yes, but unruly no. You don't have to go into each discussion daring somebody to say something about your God. Just know what you believe and be ready to share that, if and when someone asks you why you believe in God. Not only be ready to share it, but also be ready to defend it–all in meekness. In Matthew 10:16-20, Jesus explains this very thing to His disciples. He tells them they will be like sheep among wolves when they are in those faithless environments. There will be some non-Christians who will be waiting for an opportunity to tear your faith apart and make you look silly as they do it. Jesus doesn't tell His disciples to get them before they get us. He tells them to be just as wise as those faithless folks are in their responses, but gentle in how they respond. He also tells them not to worry how and if they will be able to respond, because the Holy Spirit will give them an answer at that time. Read that passage in Matthew when you have a moment. You should have a moment now, right?

Researched Incentive for Apologetics

There are several young Christians who have heard of an almighty God and of the redemptive offering (saving grace) of His Son. Still, they have several questions of who God really is and why they should believe in Him above all others. Sometimes you will ask adult Christians hard questions concerning your relationship with Christ and they won't have an answer. The problem is some of us make you think we know more about God than we really do. Then when you ask, we give you some lame answer, rather than be embarrassed for not knowing. Truth is, sometimes we just don't know.

According to George Barna, a Christian statistician and author of *Evangelism That Works*, nine out of ten Americans who say they believe in God cannot accurately define the Great Commission (it's found in Matthew 28:19-20). He states that seven out of ten have no clue what John 3:16 talks about. You do, right? Of course you do (I'll wait for you to refresh your memory, just in case, though). Why don't you try and see if Barna's statistics prove accurate. Ask the question (define the Great Commission) to ten adults you know who say they are Christians and see if the results come out about the same as Mr. Barna's. Do the same with the John 3:16 question. Many Christians (adults included) are still looking for answers to who God is and what our relationship with Him should be.

What happens when you don't have answers for what you believe to be truth and someone comes along claiming something else as truth? You're going to have a hard time deciding what to believe, aren't you? The non-truths will be so convincing you will see very little need to question their validity (whether they are fact or not). You'll just accept them as the truth, discarding what you thought to be true before. Again, those answers will look like the truth—that is if you don't know the truth.

Since the youth Bisset wrote about had not completely established their own faith in Biblical truth, they were caught in the middle of opposing faiths (in a lukewarm state as the Savior puts it). They did not have a means for giving an answer for or defending (which is what apologetics does) why they believe who God is and what He has done. Thus, they were apt to accept the answer someone else gave for who God is not and what He has not done. Their faith was shaken by the doubt surrounding it.

If you think such a thing is crazy (you know– folks can't shake your faith that way), then consider the Scriptures: "For false Christs and false prophets will arise and will show great signs and wonders, so as to mislead, if possible, even the elect (Matthew 24:24)." "The elect" Jesus refers to in this case are Christian believers. Those who have elected to believe in Christ and because of their faith, God has elected to save them. Jesus says non-truth is so convincing sometimes it can almost fool those who are grounded in Biblical truth. The keyword, though, is *almost*; but imagine what it will do to those who are not grounded. It will shake the socks off of their faith.

Atheists (those who do not believe in God) have what appears to be a strong debate for the theory of evolution. We'll discuss it later, but surely you're familiar with the theory. Although it is founded on completely unproven hypotheses (assumptions), many have accepted it as scientific fact. Most Christians have been exposed to the theory extensively in their academic studies (in the classroom), especially in their early, developmental years. If those students do not have a solid rearing (nurturing) in Biblical teaching, then they may be only one science class away from accepting something that speaks against

Scripture as the truth. If they are not ready to give an answer for why they believe what they believe, then they will have no sound doctrine by which they might debate against the other "signs and wonders" from science, philosophy, and psychology.

With facts prepared for debate, though, you can *not only* firmly stand on your own faith, but you can also discredit non-truths aimed at weakening your faith. This will place you in a position to offer the truth to those who have been misled by fallacies (non-truths). Titus 1:9 says just that; explaining sound doctrine will not only allow Christians to disprove the non-Biblical beliefs, but it also gives us a means for convincing the solicitors of evolutionism and humanism and any other "isms" (theories and philosophies) to accept Biblical truth. This is the whole purpose of apologetics–having this knowledge and being prepared to share it with others to answer their questions and refute their contradictions. Titus 1:9 says, "…holding fast the faithful word which is in accordance with the teaching, so that he will be able both to exhort [encourage] in sound doctrine and to refute [prove false] those who contradict [claim something else is the truth]." (Brackets added for clarity.) If you as a Christian student have not been given solid doctrine so you can have the wherewithal (ability) to disprove and/or convert those atheistic solicitors (those selling the idea that there is no God), then you are very prone (very likely) to be converted by them. Did you get all of that? If you can't convince them the Bible is true, they might convince you it is not.

If it seems unfathomable to you (if you're still thinking, "No way!") that a young person wanting to know the Lord could be persuaded to go another route, then consider Charles Darwin, a revolutionary in the 'religion' of evolution whom I feel certain you have heard of. Prior to writing *The Origin of Species*, the book that catapulted (tossed) evolution to the top of biological scientific theories, Darwin was studying to be (drum roll, please) in the ministry of Christ at Cambridge (Christ's Church). The guy was studying to be a minister of the gospel. If he was studying to be a minister (or priest or something), surely at one time he must have wondered who God is and how he could get to know God better. Apparently, however, he never matured in his knowledge of God in a manner that would have grounded him in the truth of the Bible and in a meaningful relationship in Christ. If he had matured in his knowledge of God, he would have had answers to some of those questions his theory posed (and still poses). He would have refuted the entire idea of evolution. Instead he questioned and questioned; and if you have any knowledge of his scientific quest, you know he never found answers to those questions. In fact, he left evidence in his writings that he eventually realized he was wrong in his theory of evolution; but we'll discuss that later. Don't rush me.

In this book you (and those training you up) will see solid Scriptural evidence of who God is. This evidence refutes what anti-Biblical writings present as evidence against Biblical truth. This book also seeks to teach you how to accept and promote the sound Christian doctrine found in the Holy Bible. Its final purpose is to move you from a lukewarm position for Jesus Christ and to make you *hot* for Him before someone else turns you *cold* against Him.

Teaching Apologetics to adolescents, however, is only a portion of the approach to giving you a Biblically sound ground to stand on. The other goal is to offer it to you in pieces that fit together systematically, so you really grasp it and will want to share it. The systematic approach should make sense. Short, verifiable steps are a system for learning employed in every area of teaching. You start with one thing. Once it is learned, you go to another which builds upon that which is learned previously. Before you know it you have a complete knowledge transfer (you're smarter). The process leaves out some of the intricate details of the matter, which are not necessary for ground-level learning. The intricate (complicated) details can be addressed once you learn the basic concepts.

The apostle Paul gives us this teaching process in some of his writings to the Christians of his day. Two excellent examples of this principle may be found in Scriptures where Paul addresses Christians on how to train in Biblical truths. First in 1 Timothy 1:4, "…nor to pay attention to myths and endless genealogies, which give rise to mere speculation rather than furthering the administration of God which is by faith;" then in Titus 3:9, "But avoid foolish controversies and genealogies and strife and disputes about the Law, for they are unprofitable and worthless. In both cases, Paul warns us to not get caught up in the intricate details of the knowledge of God (things that spark human interest or debate–genealogies, speculation, controversies, and disputes about the way things used to be under the law). Instead, we keep with the basics and build a foundation from which you can teach others about God (or as stated by Paul, "Further the administration of God").

Incentive from Surveys, Tests, and Observation

The systematic portion to this approach to preparing you to hold to and share your faith is universally accepted. That means not many people will argue against it. Some folks, however, have suggested that the theology contained here may be too intense for you. I was once somewhat reprimanded for (pulled aside and told to stop) going 'so deep' with some of the kids I was teaching. I was actually asked to stick with the very basic teaching principles of an online Sunday School curriculum, which was very elementary (this was a classroom of teenagers–the majority of them in high school or already in college). Of course, I respectfully protested the reprimand. I wasn't rude or arrogant or anything. I just made an appeal. My argument was the youth already knew and were bored with the elementary stories they had been taught over the years. The argument was *not* that the basic accounts of Biblical history found in those Sunday School curriculums were inappropriate for those teenagers. My argument was they already knew it so it was not uninteresting. It wasn't triggering Spiritual growth in them. It is the same thing Bisset concluded in his research. Those kids' knowledge of God was not experiencing growth so neither was their faith.

Listen, if a thing stops growing, then it has started experiencing a slow and steady death. This holds true for plants; it holds true for humans/animals; and it holds true for our faith. If their faith had stopped growing–guess what? Yep. It was dying. The information in that curriculum was too basic to nurture those teens. It would not keep them grounded when evaluated against 'other information' they would encounter in their college or early adult years.

At this juncture (at this point), it was best for me to not theorize a belief that youth could and wanted to understand serious things of God (i.e., deeper theology than the story of Moses parting the Red Sea, etc). I felt certain they could understand this theology as much as they understood science and algebraic equations in the school classroom. Rather than leave it as theory, I decided to test the idea that young folks could and wanted to learn at a deeper level. I decided I would use the concept found in this book in Youth Sunday School and Bible Study classes. So, that's what I did. I tested my theory (if I may borrow another term from science) to see if youth truly did want to go deeper in their knowledge of God. I tested it in two different churches that were totally different in their modus operandi (how they did things).

The first *experiment* was in Bible Study with African American, Caucasian, Latino, and multi-ethnic/multi-racial youth of ages ranging from thirteen to eighteen plus. One youth posed the question (in a previous session), "If jealousy is a sin for us, why is it not a sin for God?" She had heard the question on the radio (a non-Christian station), which a caller asked while reciting Scripture from the Old

Testament referencing God as a jealous God. The easy way out of that question would have been to answer, "God is God. He can do what He wants to do. If He can allow Moses to part the Red Sea when nobody else could, then He can be jealous while no one else can." There is certainly truth in that, but it's not the whole truth.

Rather than give the typical answer of "God is God," however, I conducted a little research, which uncovered a theologically sound answer to her hard question about God. The answer was presented to the class at the next session. It was very simple. The words of that passage of Scripture had been taken out of context (misinterpreted). Every Hebrew word I found in the Old Testament used for describing God as a jealous God meant something totally different from what the modern western society (which includes the United States) understands jealousy to be.

You should have seen how intensely they listened as the Biblical answer was carefully explained (in as youthful a context as I could muster). It was amazing. Some of their faces just showed they were saying inside, "Aha!" or "So that's it!" No one was talking to others or playing with things or reading or doing homework as I had observed them doing in the past while we studying lessons in Biblical history. This clearly revealed they not only could understand deeper theology, but they really wanted to have an answer to give when asked hard questions about God.

A second test of this 'theory' that young people could and would involve themselves in deeper theology came during Children's Church with African American kids of ages ranging from ten to twelve. The lesson was on the importance of studying to know the truth. The text was 2 Timothy 2:15, "Study to shew thyself approved unto God, a workman that needeth not to be ashamed, rightly dividing the word of truth (KJV)." I used the King James Version of the Bible specifically, because the kids recognized this passage of Scripture from their Bible Study on Wednesday nights. We had a lot of discussions on things they had learned in science and how those things compared to Biblical truth.

They were very engrossed (engaged) in the lesson, because they could really relate to the topics. They were familiar with the Scripture, since it was their theme Scripture from AWANA Club (Wednesday night Bible Study). They were familiar with the scientific terms, because they had all covered them in science classes time after time. In fact (sad to note), they were more interactive with the questions and statements about cell formation, archeology, evolution, and the like, because they were more familiar with science than with Scripture (only because they had been exposed to it more often and more intensely.) When I explained to them how science actually proved evolution false, they became even more interested in Scripture. Then once I explained creationism, according to Scripture, they could make the correlation (connection) between truth and non-truth and why it is important to know the truth.

I was just tickled at the excitement one of the eleven-year-olds showed in knowing how to refute evolution. She expressed she did not believe "that stuff" anyway. Her statement (based on faith) was impressive, but think how much stronger her faith would be and her ability to resist non-truth now that she was armed with a truth to accompany her faith.

The ultimate shocker came at the end of the class, however, when I denoted (indicated) the discussion was over. Remember, those were TEN to TWELVE year-olds. They just started clapping and everyone in the class had a satisfied look on their face as if they had feasted on the Bread of Life. TEN to TWELVE year-olds! Offering ovation (applause) to God for His truth!! Young boys usually needing to be reminded to focus were intently listening and responding. Young girls were answering or nodding their heads in acknowledgement of understanding instead of giggling among themselves or fumbling around in their purses for lip gloss or a half piece of uneaten peppermint.

It amazed me how God confirmed that His Word is definitely comprehensible (understandable) and sought after by youth. We old folks just need to take the time to help you understand it. Just those two experiments convinced me youth desire a deeper understanding of God. It is also interesting that the two groups were for the most part a perfect representation of what experts feel make up the age group for adolescents—ages ten to eighteen. They all came from different backgrounds and yet all still had the same hunger for the truth of

Scripture. From this, I am convinced that you can and will grasp sound theology and you will hold on to it and when your faith is challenged, it will not be shaken.

Conclusion

Tom Bisset really sparked my interest with his book, *Why Christian Kids Leave the Faith*. I was glad to see the end of his research proved that most who do drop out (as he puts it), come back later in life. This proves (not that we as Christians would doubt) the Scripture found in Proverbs 22:6 says, "Train up a child in the way he should go, even when he is old he will not depart from it," is very correct. This means Mr. Bisset's question should be, "Why do Christian kids periodically check out of the faith?"

Again, I'm not trying to dispute with Mr. Bisset over his point. His point is very clear and I agree with it fully: There is something terribly wrong when Christian kids have an identity problem with who they are in Christ, such that they are swayed so often and so easily. The intent here is not to question if Mr. Bisset offers valuable information on why they leave. He does. The intent, again, is to propose the question from another angle: "How we can make Christian kids never leave?"

The Other SAT process will begin with understanding who the God of the Bible is. That is the logical beginning to answering your questions about God and strengthening your faith in Him. *The Other SAT* will discuss how to help others to know and accept the God of the Bible. Helping others accept God was the goal from the start of

Christianity and it will be the goal until the end time as we know it. *The Other SAT* will discuss how to prove Biblical truth–not for your own sake–but for the sake of those who don't believe. Some non-truths attempt to prove the Bible incorrect, thus claim to have a different truth. *The Other SAT* will demonstrate how to recognize and reprove non-truth. You need to be able to recognize a non-truth, so you will not unknowingly accept it as truth. *The Other SAT* will discuss how to trust the Bible as truth. This is the faith required to have a personal relationship with God through Jesus Christ. Finally, *The Other SAT* will discuss how to apply the knowledge of God. The most effective way to obtain, share, prove, and trust the knowledge of God is to apply it in your own life. God makes ways for youth (everyone for that matter) to know Him. Applying that knowledge in your lives compels others to seek the God of the Bible and demonstrates concrete evidence of Him.

You will certainly be confronted by those in the realm of academia (schools, colleges, and universities) and other walks of life who simply do not believe in an almighty God. Some will just deny Him, but others will attack even the idea of such a God. You will need to have a response for the assaults on Bible-based Christianity and the attempts to explain it away with humankind's philosophies.

To produce a horde (crowd) of mindless militants against secular education is *not* the goal of this book. Knowledge is a wonderful thing. I have attended secular colleges and believe my secular education has made life better–to God be the glory. I really encourage you to do the same. There is endless good a secular education can do for any person.

I have no desire, with this book, to place a wedge between Christians and non-Christians. Christians should love to see each of their unsaved friends and loved ones come to know Jesus Christ as their own personal savior. Our relationship with non-Christians keeps hope in place for seeing them come to know Christ one day. The Bible gives a clear example of that in Paul's teachings when he talks about becoming all things to all people so he might cause some to be saved. Interrelationships between Christians and non-Christians are essential in proving the realness of God and spreading the gospel of Jesus Christ.

This book was not designed to eat away at your dreams in life (your secular goals) or tear down relationships with or respect for others, either. If your desire is to be a doctor, be a doctor. If your desire is to be a lawyer, be that lawyer. If your desire is to be the next world's greatest athlete, do what it takes to be the next world's greatest athlete; and make lots of friends doing it. You should never let anyone discourage you against reaching your goals.

Systematic Adolescent Theology intends to better equip you, as you go to the next stage of life, to maintain your faith in what can prove to be faithless environments. This book has two primary goals. Its first goal can be found in Colossians 2:8. We want to "See to it that no one takes you captive through hollow and deceptive philosophy, which depends on human tradition and the basic principles of this world rather than on Christ (NIV)." Its second goal can be found in 2

Corinthians 10:5. "We are destroying speculations and every lofty thing raised up against the knowledge of God…"

Now; let us begin our knowledge of God.

2 OBTAINING KNOWLEDGE OF GOD

You must have a knowledge of God if you are going to have a relationship with Him (Rf. John 10:27)

Not Knowing God

What you know about God defines your theology. In other words, your knowledge of God is your theology. It is what you have studied and found out about God. You must have knowledge of God if you are going to have a relationship with Him. You must have a sound theology if you're going to be ready to give an account of what you believe about God (as 1 Peter 3:15 instructs us). This does not mean you have to make memorable statements and have clever insights about God's Word like those great theologians (those who spend many years studying and knowing God's Word) have displayed over the years. Having a sound theology simply means you understand and agree with the basic Biblical truths about God and Christianity. You must have a sound theology before you can give an account of who God is. We will go through and gather enough information to provide you with a sound theology, but first let me share a discussion I had with a couple of friends from work. This may help you understand the importance of having a sound theology.

Discussion Among Friends

The importance of having a sound theology became extremely evident to me when I found myself in a discussion with two individuals who would not recognize themselves with a 'brand of religion' (especially Christianity), even though they both recognized there is a God. For the purpose of anonymity (to keep from revealing who they are), we'll label those two folks Person1 and Person2. Person1 recognized there is one true God, but Person2 just felt the universe was god. Person1 left a lot of ambiguity (uncertainty) in their explanation of God and Person2 just did not believe one single entity (one person or thing) could be in authority over every other person and thing.

The discussion began when Person1 said, "I just threw it out there and let the universe decide what to do with it." I asked Person1 just what they thought "the universe" could do with it. I was trying to stir up some healthy discussion on belief systems and worldviews. (I saw this as an opportunity to witness or explain Christianity.) Eventually our discussion got to the point where I could ask the question, "So you believe the universe is a god." Person1 said, "I believe in God, I just like to use a generic term, so I don't offend others who don't believe like I believe." Person1 must have known that Person2 believed in the universe as a god; therefore Person1 used 'universe' as their generic term so they wouldn't offend Person2.

Person1 sort of had the right idea. We as Christians should definitely do our best not to offend others with our beliefs. Jesus teaches us not to offend in Luke 17:1-4. In the passage of Scripture sited in Luke, He teaches we should never allow our offenses to block others from wanting to become a Christian. The Greek word for offend in those Scriptures (*skandalizo*) actually means "to put a stumbling block or impediment [obstacle] in the way of" or (the one I like) "to cause a person to begin to distrust and desert one whom he ought to trust and obey." (Brackets added for clarification.)

We can't approach non-Christians with an attitude that we are more worthy of God's grace than they. We most certainly are not. Likewise, we can't dislike or mistreat them just because they have a different belief system than us. In fact, we are instructed by Christ to do just the opposite. (Read Matt 5:43-47 and Luke 6:27-35 when you have the chance.) Making non-Christians feel unworthy of God's grace or mistreating them would probably make them never want to become a Christian (block them from ever knowing Christ as Savior) or cause them not to trust Christ as they should. This is Jesus' point in teaching us not to offend them.

For the record, Jesus also instructs Christians (in Matthew 17:24-27) to not offend each other with different ways of showing our affection for God or our duty to God. We don't all have to go to the same church, be a part of the same denomination or abide by the same church bylaws (rules). If an individual or church honors God one way and another honors Him a different way, it should not cause conflict among us. (Now, not everything honors God, but we can determine from the Bible what does and what doesn't.) Christians can have different ways of honoring God, provided those ways of honoring God align with how Scriptures state we should honor Him. We should not be offensive towards others because they do things a little different than we. By offending each other, we trip up one another, thus hindering each other's walk of faith.

It is clear from Jesus' teachings that we should do our best *not* to offend. However, we must also not compromise what we know as

Biblical truth in the process. That means we should not hide our knowledge of God or lay it aside and accept others' beliefs, just to appease (satisfy) them. The Apostle Paul teaches this in 1 Corinthians 9:19-22. He shows us how he would associate with others in their customs (he would take part in their cultural activities) as long as it did not cause him to compromise his own knowledge of what God requires in our relationship with Him. Paul would hang out with them, but would not do stuff Christians shouldn't do or believe what Christians shouldn't believe.

In their attempt to not offend Person2, Person1 may have given them the wrong impression of who God is by referring to God as 'the Universe'. Person1 tried to relate to Person2 according to Person2's belief system, but Person1 compromised their Christian belief system. They may have reinforced Person2's idea that the universe is a god. Although it was probably not intentional, it was a compromise.

Paul did not disrespect people in any way that would offend them and cause them not to accept Christianity. However, he did not mislead anyone into thinking he was anything other than Christian. He always acknowledged God for who God is. He did as Jesus taught in the passage referenced in Luke above. All Christians should follow that example.

By the time Person1, Person2 and I got to a point in the discussion where we could address issues with this generic labeling of God or appointing everything that exists as God, I was bubbling over with excitement. I really wanted to get them to know God from the Bible's perspective. It seemed at that point, all they had were their opinions of Him. Sometimes opinions are totally opposite of fact.

Person1 seemed to believe we can't really know God enough to say who is right about Him and who is wrong. So, they figured everybody could be right in their own way. At least that is the way they presented it during our discussion. Again, perhaps they were just trying not to offend Person2. I applaud their effort; however, I do not recommend their method. The approach to God Person1 was taking is called the agnostic theist approach. Agnostic theists believe there is one true God, but humans have no way of obtaining concrete (visible; understandable) knowledge of that God. They also don't believe we can have a personal relationship with God. They believe He just created us and left us alone. They just accept the fact that there is a God and that's good enough for them. Well, that's not Biblically correct thinking (it's bad theology). God wants a personal relationship with us. He makes us aware of this all throughout the Bible.

Person2 just felt like all is god. They felt everything in the universe sustains (takes care of) itself, therefore (by default, perhaps) the universe is god. Since all is a part of the universe, all is a part of that god (as they believe it). The belief Person2 held is called Pantheism. Pantheists believe the physical universe is God.

I wanted a chance to introduce the God of the Bible to them, but most of my time was spent correcting Person2. Person2 presented a much distorted view of Christianity–as they saw it. Person2 must have seen a lot of folks professing (saying they are) Christians doing a lot of non-Christ-like things. The term, "you Christians", was such a recurring statement (they said it over and over) I had to spend most of my time defending Biblical Christianity.

Eventually the discussion came to a point to where everyone could make their closing statements. It was lunch time, so we had a very limited time to discuss each topic that came up. Person2 made the argument that Christianity divides. "Just look at the amount of division within the Christian 'religion'," they said. My argument against that was they had seen denominational differences, not division. As stated before, we as churches can do things differently without being divided.

After all the discussion, however, it was apparent Person2 would not accept Christianity because they felt it held such a singularity in its view of God. That was Person2's conclusion. Person1 was still just passive (would not openly take a stand for Christianity or against). That is a very dangerous stance to take. Although Alexander Hamilton originally came up with the statement, Malcolm X is also quoted for saying: "A man who stands for nothing will fall for anything." Hanging around on middle ground is a very dangerous thing.

Person2 did not like the fact that Christianity does not allow other beliefs to become a part of it. There is a reason why Christianity remains by itself, but we'll discuss that momentarily. Before Person2 would accept Christianity, it would have to reconcile itself (that is, it would have to in some way agree or compromise) with others' views of God. That meant it would have to compromise with Buddhism, Islamic beliefs, Judaism, Naturalism, Relativism, Evolutionism, Pantheism, Panentheism, Deism, Agnosticism or any other "ism" out there claiming to hold the truth about God. Person2 felt Christianity just would not allow harmony among those with differing belief systems. It does not play well with other religions. They maintained (their final argument was) Christianity is just too narrow-minded for them.

I disagreed–first, with their statement that Christians could not live in harmony with non-Christians. My best case for that would have been that Jesus offered salvation to the ones who hung Him on the cross. Their sole purpose for nailing Him to the cross was His belief system did not fit theirs. Yet, He still wanted a relationship with them. If that does not exemplify (demonstrate) ability to live in harmony, despite differing worldviews, I don't know what does. But, of course that argument would not work for them, because it is based on the singular idea that what the Bible says about this Jesus Christ guy is true (again, that's too narrow-minded for some folks). So, I didn't make this statement aloud. I just humored myself with the thought.

I did speak out on my second observation, though. My second thought was this: The fact that we could have our conversation over lunch and return to work in the same friendly manner in which we left was proof enough that those with differing worldviews (including us

Christians) could live together in harmony. For some reason, they didn't argue that point. How could they, right?

After that, I presented them with my final case. Here are what some of my closing statements were:

Regardless of whether you agree or disagree if Christianity is the only truth for knowing God, you have to know that there can only be one truth. Therefore, there is no way to reconcile (compromise, straddle the fence, waffle, hover between, or be lukewarm about) the differences in opposing beliefs. When all is said and done, only one can be true making the others false. That means you will have to hold to one of those beliefs as truth and deem (consider) the others false. It all goes back to the first principle of logic.

Both Person1 and Person2 could agree with applying the first principle of logic to our debate. That's because it is not a Biblical concept, but rather a philosophical theorem—perhaps addressed best by Aristotle. Don't fret. It's okay to go outside the Bible when trying to reach people who don't know the Bible. Jesus did it.

When He taught Jews, He often quoted Scripture or traditional Jewish statements. He would often begin a lesson with "It is written…" or "You have heard it said…" while addressing someone who was familiar with the Jewish culture. He spoke concerning Scriptures when teaching in the synagogues or among the religious leaders. However, often when He taught to those who did not know the Jewish Culture (the Gentiles); He would use stories (parables) to explain Biblical messages. His listeners understood the themes he used, because those themes involved current events or cultural habits with which they were familiar. Since the people understood those themes, Jesus could relate Biblical principles through those themes. The people could then understand the gospel message he associated those stories with.

I used the first principle of logic with Person1 and Person2, because I knew they were familiar with them. They were both well-educated in the secular academic system. I knew I could use the first principle of logic to introduce them to Biblical principles. Person1 and Person2 did not debate with that. They knew those principles hold true in anything logical. They also knew within the first principle of logic lies the law of non-contradiction (LNC). There are some very deep and philosophical definitions for LNC out there. In simple terms, it states that an argument cannot end with two opposing truths. If 'A' is true then 'non-A' (anything that argues against A) cannot be true.

This is the logic used in developing theories. In developing theories you cannot end with two opposing truths and say that you have proven your theory. Also with theories, you start with a single truth concerning that theory and work out any non-truths opposing that theory. Throughout the process you can't deviate (move away) from the truth, so that in the end what you wound up with will still be the truth. If you wind up with two opposing arguments concerning your theory, you can trace them backwards to see which one remains true; consequently making the other false.

It's the same principle you use when working out those long algebra problems (polynomials–in case you've been sleeping in math class). If you get to the end and your answer doesn't match what the answer key says it is you have opposing arguments as to what solves that algebra problem. Of course, you can almost be positive that *your* argument is the incorrect argument. You can then work your way back and figure out where you went astray. You have made a statement somewhere in there that is not true. Something contradicts what you started with and there can be no contradictions in the equation. With the answer key, you know your answer's wrong and can go back to re-work it. Don't you wish you could have the answer key *before* you take those algebra exams?

The LNC operates on that principle. It works in math. It works in science. It works in philosophy. It even works in knowing God. The only difference in knowing math, science, and philosophy and in knowing God is that God always offers the answer key in his Word! So, you can constantly check the key and see if you are solving your problems as you should. You don't have to wait until the end. At that point, if you're wrong–you've already flunked.

Staying with the Biblical Account of God

Now, back to why Christianity chooses to stand alone–as the discussion relates to belief systems. Let's use the example of water, again, to see if we can make this clear. (Get it–water, clear?) Anyway, take the fact that two parts hydrogen and one part oxygen ($H2O1$)

make up the chemical elements found in water. If you keep mixing those two chemical elements together in those proportions (2 to 1), regardless of the quantity–five ounces, five gallons or five oceans–you can ascertain (be sure) that you still have water; based on the truth you started with: two parts (or two-thirds) hydrogen mixed with one part (or one-third) oxygen is water. After all the mixing is complete, you can measure what you have, based on the formula and–wallah!!! You have water.

If anybody changes the formula of the mixture on you along the way (no matter how slight the change), you will come up with something totally different than water. They can add just one more part oxygen to your two parts hydrogen and you have something totally different–hydrogen peroxide. H2O1 = water, but H2O2 = hydrogen peroxide. In case you don't know what hydrogen peroxide is (usually simply referred to as peroxide); it's the almost clear, fizzy liquid poured onto cuts to kill germs. Yeah, it burns like crazy! It is also used on hair to bleach it white (or blonde or something). Some folks even use it to whiten their teeth.

That's a lot different than the substance we started with, isn't it? Is it safe to make this minor substitution in our formula? And would you dare substitute the original product (water) with this new product (peroxide) in some of your food or beverage recipes? What about your soup? Think it would taste the same with peroxide as with water? Would you make Kool-Aid® with H2O2 instead of H2O1? Yuck! If anyone ever offers you Kool-Aid® made with peroxide, don't drink the Kool-Aid®!

The same goes for the Christian worldview. If anyone uses anything other than the formula found in Biblical truth to tell you who God is and what a Christian's relationship with Him should be, don't drink the Kool-Aid®! If someone mixes Biblical Christian truth with any other belief system, they no longer have Christianity. They have something much different. Just like peroxide in Kool-Aid®, they have created something that is just awful. Yuck!

When all is said and done, all those different beliefs will be measured based on the formula for truth. Only one can be true. The others must be false. We have a fine example of this in Revelation 3:12-16 where the church at Pergamum was warned of folks mixing other elements into the gospel formula. The warning was that they now had a bad formula brewing. If they didn't stop, they would have a terrible price to pay at the end. But, why wait until the end to see if we have mixed the right elements into our message of truth? We know the formula. The Bible offers it with a perfectly laid-out answer key. Why mix it incorrectly knowing you no longer have the true formula for knowing God when you do so?

That is how Christianity remains Christianity. It keeps the same formula or the same recipe regardless of how much stirring takes place—no matter how big the batch grows. It may be served up in different ways. Just as you can be exposed to water in different formats (a liquid, a gas [steam] and a solid [ice]), you can be exposed to Christianity in different formats. One Christian church may do things one way and another differently, but they all send the same Gospel message.

True Christianity does not mix in other worldviews (beliefs) so that it might reconcile itself (agree) with them. I suppose that's why it gets labeled as having too singular a basis for its beliefs (it sort of gets labeled as being narrow-minded). Christianity is not a narrow-minded belief system. It just chooses *not* to wait until the mixing is done to determine if it still has the true formula for water (in this case living water!). It chooses to stick with the formula (truth), so there is no question what the final product will be.

We as Christians will have to decide to stay with the formula if we are to be ready to give the correct answer for why we believe in what we believe. It doesn't matter how many new and exciting looking recipes come about for who God is and about humankind's relationship to Him. Only the original recipe works. And that's the recipe Jesus gave us.

In many ways, our Christian belief system differs greatly from other belief systems. They are like oil and water and simply will not mix. You can try and stir them together if you want, but eventually, however, the oil will float to the top. If you've ever paid attention to oil on top of water, it does not stay there forever. In the case of still water (such as a pond or lake), all you need to do is set a match to it and it will burn off.

Otherwise, you can wait for ripples to form, either from wind or other disturbances, and the oil will find its way to the shores and cling onto rocks and plants and sand, until eventually you have pure water again. In the case of flowing water (such as streams or rivers), the oil will eventually do the same thing as it makes its way downstream or down river. It will cling onto rocks and plants and sand along the way, until eventually you have pure water again. Either way; in the end we will have pure water, again. Matthew 24:35, Mark 13:31, and Luke 21:33 all record Jesus in saying, "Heaven and earth shall all pass away, but my words shall not pass away." All non-truth will eventually get washed away, but God's Word will remain true.

It is amazing how well this metaphor (symbolism) of the properties and chemical makeup of water explains the importance of staying with the recipe if we are going to maintain the truth. When Jesus introduced His truth to a woman at a well, He refers to His gospel message as water ("living water" in John 4:10). John 4:13-14 states, "Jesus answered and said to her, 'Everyone who drinks of this water [the water in the well: H2O1] will thirst again; but whoever drinks of the water [gospel] that I will give him shall never thirst; but the water [gospel] that I will give him will become in him a well of water [truth] springing up to eternal life.'" (Brackets added for clarity.) Jesus refers to his offering of salvation and his teachings (aka gospel) as water in this referenced passage and later as the truth in other passages of Scripture (for example, later in John 8:32 and John 14:6). When we accept the gospel truth, it just keeps bubbling up in us so we never thirst again for what is true. We don't have to spend the rest of our lives searching for a different truth (like what the unattainable intellectual honesty suggests is out there somewhere).

It was clear as well water that Person2 was still thirsting for some truth in their worldview. They had a lot of unanswered questions and unsupported theories and all with an uncertain end. They could neither trace their arguments back to truth nor could they finalize them with truth, because their arguments either did not begin with the truth or strayed far from it. I would compare that to a math problem which can't be solved. You'd be racking your brain to solve it, but to no avail (you wouldn't get anywhere with it).

It must be really uncomfortable to go through life wondering what the truth really is and where it began and where it will eventually lead. Without truth, what does a person have to trust in? What does a person have to turn to? What do they have to hope for? Christians know the truth of the Gospel and we should want to stick with it. Truth is the source to life which frees us from thirsting (or searching) for something that is just not there.

Knowing God

So, our first object of study is: Who is God? This is a good place to start, because many theistic religions (i.e., religions that believe in only one God) claim the God of the bible as their God, but have differing views of exactly who He is. Their views, in some cases, clash (disagree) really bad with what the Bible says. There are some groups who even label themselves as Christians, but still have differing views of who

Christ is and what His relationship to God is. This is the reason for the confusion among atheists (those who do not believe there is a God) and others such as Person2 previously discussed. This is one of the reasons Person2 did not want to be associated with the designation (title or label) Christian and Person1 did not want to offend Person2 by being called a Christian.

The Bible is clear on who God is from beginning to end. In fact, it says He is the beginning and the end. It is so clear, about the identity of God; it's hard to understand why so many people misinterpret it. It makes it seem almost certain that the misinterpretations are intentional. Well, intentional or not, it is dangerous to promote God as anyone but who He really is. So, we will search the Scriptures to see Him as we should.

The Bible teaches that God has always existed. It also teaches He exists in three distinct entities (persons): God the Father, God the Son, and God the Holy Spirit (also referred to as the Holy Ghost). Even though they are three separate entities, the Bible clearly exhibits (reveals) they are still one Sovereign (superior/absolute) Being. The theological way to state this is to say God is a triune God. Theologians refer to God in whole as the Trinity. This is perhaps the most difficult attribute (characteristic) of God to understand and it is even more difficult to explain. Because it is so difficult to understand, we must (until we fully understand it) just believe what the Bible says about the triune nature of God. Some will argue because the word trinity does not appear in the Bible, it is just a man-made concept. They will argue that it's a theological theory and not a biblical fact. Well, the Bible does not mention the word trinity, but it gives all the facts needed to determine that God is a triune God. Folks can use any word the wish to label it with; the evidence is clearly there.

God the Father

The third verse in the Bible (Genesis 1:3) illustrates God acting as the Creator or the Sovereign Being (often referred to in Scriptures as the Father). It reads, "Then God said, 'Let there be light'; and there was light." God as the Sovereign Being began to speak all things into existence. Can you imagine that kind of power? He just spoke the Word and things began to happen.

The Bible later illustrates the Fatherly qualities of God. Just like a good father wants what is best for his child, God wants what is best for His children. By the way, everyone who believes in Jesus Christ are adopted into the family of God, thus are His children (rf. Romans 8:16-17). The goodness of an earthly father doesn't even compare to that of God, the heavenly Father. The Bible states so in Matthew 7:9-11.

9"...what man is there among you who, when his son asks for a loaf, will give him a stone? 10"Or if he asks for a fish, he will not give him a snake, will he? 11"If you then, being evil, know how to give good gifts to your children, how much more will your Father who is in heaven give what is good to those who ask Him!

Jesus is the speaker in this passage of Scripture. He wants His listeners to understand how much God the Father loves them. Here He speaks of an earthly father as evil. The Greek word used here for evil is *peneros* (pronounced pon-ay-ros') and it means "of a bad nature or condition."

Jesus is not being mean and calling everyone devils. He is explaining the nature or condition of humankind as a whole. You can see this condition of humankind demonstrated all throughout the book of Romans. The Scripture in Romans 3:23 states that all have sinned and fall short of the glory of God. "Fall short" (*hustereo* in Greek) means lacks.

Humankind lacks the glory God created it with. This is a bad condition. This condition is due to the sin humankind inherited from the first man, Adam. The passage of Scripture in Romans 5:18-19 explains the bad nature or condition of humankind, which was inherited through the first man's sin. The Scripture in Romans 6:23 states that this nature or condition deserves death. Jesus is showing us even though earthly fathers have this bad nature or condition (so bad it deserves death), they still know how to care for and nurture their own. I don't mean to sound too much like a preacher with this one, but just check the newspaper, news on TV, or just listen to folks talk around you when out in public. It won't take long to encounter this bad nature or condition in folks.

Now, the passage of Scripture in Romans 5:18-19 explains the bad nature or condition of humankind, but it also talks about the care and nurture God the Father has to offer. It says that although one man caused this bad condition on humankind, God the Father made provision (prepared a way) for the condition to be changed for the better. Likewise, although Romans 6:23 says humankind's nature or condition deserves death, God the Father (in spite of that) offers the gift of life. Because God did not want the condition of humankind to cause death to anyone (2 Peter 3:9 states this), He offered the gift of life. Knowing God the Father, the first person of the triune God, offers hope that we can escape the bad condition in which sin has positioned us.

God the Son

Colossians 2:6-10 shows us Jesus as God the Son. Verse 9 states, "For in Him all the fullness of Deity [attributes of God] dwells in bodily form." (Brackets added for clarity.) He became a human being for one reason–to pay the debt (wages discussed above–Romans 6:23) for sin. The debt for sin had to be paid. God had established that. God had also established the cost for sin; and He decided to pay its price. He decided He would pay the debt so we would no longer remain in the bad condition sin has placed us. We no longer have to be separated from Him by sin. Death as used in Romans 6:23 means separation in Greek–*thanatos*. So, death in this case meant our separation from God. The position of sin is separation from God.

Since God determined that humankind had to be separated from Him because of sin, the only One to reconcile (bring back together) God and humankind was God Himself. Jesus Christ, God the Son, did just that. John 3:16 makes this clear. Jesus, through His death and resurrection (coming back to life) paid back the debt of sin for all humankind. Romans 5:8 says that while people were still sinners, Christ died for them. He abolished (did away with) the death penalty for sin. Humankind and God no longer have to be separated because of sin. Of course, one would have to choose to accept God's offer of reconciliation. In order to do that, they would have to believe in Jesus as the Son.

Now, anyone who believes Jesus Christ is Lord and that God raised Him from the dead can be saved from their sins. Their relationship to God the Father can be restored through faith in God the Son. The passage in Romans 10:9 tells us this. It states, "That if you confess with your mouth Jesus as Lord, and believe in your heart that God raised Him from the dead, you will be saved."

Knowing and believing in God the Son, the second person of the triune God, completes our reconciliation with God. That reconciliation with God is referred to as salvation in Romans 10:10. Salvation in ancient Greek (*soteria*–so-tay-ree'-ah) meant deliverance; safety. Salvation (or to be saved as we Christians often say) means we are delivered out of (or safe from) the penalty of sin. We are no longer separated from God because of sin, but reconciled with Him because of Christ Jesus.

A key passage of Scripture tying God the Son (Jesus) to God the Father (the Creator/Sovereign Being) is John 1:1-3 & 14.

> [1]In the beginning was the Word, and the Word was with God, and the Word was God. [2]He was in the beginning with God. [3]All things came into being through Him, and apart from Him nothing came into being that has come into being. [14]*And the Word became flesh, and dwelt among us*, and we saw His glory, glory as of the only begotten from the Father, full of grace and truth. (Emphasis added.)

If you read the entire chapter of John 1, you'll see John is referring to Jesus as "the Word." It is clear that God and Christ are one.

God the Holy Spirit

Jesus promised the Holy Spirit to all who believe in Him. John 7:39 explains, "But this spake he of the Spirit, which they that believe on him should receive." Jesus gives the Holy Spirit as a helper to improve our knowledge of God through Him, as well as to help maintain our relationship with God through Him. John 14:26 states,

> But the *Comforter*, which is the Holy Ghost, whom the Father will send in my name, he shall teach you all things, and bring all things to your remembrance, whatsoever I have said unto you. (Emphasis added.)

A key passage of Scripture tying God the Son (Jesus) to God the Spirit (The Holy Spirit) is John 14:11-20; specifically verses 11, 16, and 20.

> [11]Believe me that I am in the Father, and the Father in me. Or else believe me for the very works' sake. [16]"I will ask the Father, and He will give you another *Helper*, that He may be with you forever; [20]"In that day you will know that I am in My Father, and you in Me, and I in you. (Emphasis added.)

You should understand the "Helper" is the Holy Spirit (or Holy Ghost) as clarified in Acts 1:4, 5 and 8.

> [4]And, being assembled together with them, commanded them that they should not depart from Jerusalem, but wait for the promise of the Father, which, saith he, ye have heard of me. [5]For John truly baptized with water; but ye shall be baptized with the Holy Ghost not many days hence. [8]But ye shall receive power, after that the Holy Ghost is come upon you.

A key passage of Scripture tying God the Father, to God the Son (Jesus) and to God the Spirit (The Holy Spirit) is 1 John 3:23-24.

> [23]And this is his [God's] commandment, That we should believe on the name of his Son Jesus Christ, and love one another, as he gave us commandment. [24]And he that keepeth his [Jesus'] commandments dwelleth in him [Jesus], and he [Jesus] in him [the Christian]. And hereby we know that he [Jesus] abideth in us, by the

73

Spirit [Holy Spirit] which he [God] hath given us. (Brackets added for clarity.)

Knowing God the Holy Spirit gives us the means by which we can maintain the right relationship with the triune God.

I know this section may seem a little preachy to you and maybe even a little complicated (or a lot), but it is important for you to understand our relationship with God through Jesus Christ. Read through it a few times if necessary. Get a good Christian teacher (pastor, Sunday school teacher, etc.) to help you with it if you need to. Ask them to try and make it plain. The trinity can be very difficult to understand. If I were to try and allegorize (symbolize; paint a mental picture of) it I would do it this way:

My name is James Gamble. I am just a man. I am just one man. I am the father of James, II and Marcinda Gamble (J.J. and Marcy). I created them (sort of). I love them dearly. I am the son of Sam and Martha Gamble. They created me (sort of). I love them dearly. I am the comforter of Lucinda Gamble (Lu). I will never leave her or forsake her. I love her dearly. I am James the father, James the son, and James the comforter (synonymous to Holy Spirit some places in the Bible, but only an allegory here). I am just a man. I am just one man.

I am one man and I love them all dearly; but I don't manifest my love to them all in the same way. I have never felt obligated to say "Yes, sir" or "Yes, ma'am" to J.J. and Marcy. I always will to Sam and Martha. I have never felt compelled to say, "koochie, koochie, koo" to Sam or Martha. I have done so quite a few times to J.J. and Marcy – not so much since they've become adults. I have said some things to Lu in the name of love that would creep out either of the others if I said it to them. I love them all dearly as one man; but I manifest my love to them all through this triune characteristic of mine. If I, being just a man, can manifest my love for them in three different ways, how much easier must it be for God to manifest His love for us in three different ways?

1 Peter 1:2 demonstrates God's triune character in one verse. So do Matthew 28:19 and 2 Corinthians 13:14. The greatest difference in our triune character and God's, though, is ours' cannot be physically manifested (observable) as God's is in the Father, the Son, and the Holy Spirit. My three-part presentation of myself was symbolic. God's three-part presentation is real.

The understanding that God is a triune God may be the greatest reason different theistic religions cannot reconcile their beliefs. In other words, this is why some religions (those claiming the Bible as their base) do not agree with Christianity. This is the division within 'religions' Person2 alluded to (hinted at) in the opening discussion. The division stems (comes) mainly from the fact that many religions refuse to acknowledge what the aforementioned (and other) passages of Scripture state about the triune character of God. Those religions who do not accept the truth of a triune God have changed the formula the Bible has given us for who God is. They are not being true to the Scriptures from which they base their belief system. I guess we could say there is no intellectual honesty happening with them.

The divisions are not within Christianity itself as Person2 cited incorrectly. It is among those versions of theism that claim the Bible as their basis, but do not fully hold to Bible principles (truths). True Christianity bases its principles on Biblical truth. So, there can be no disagreement in the basic beliefs for Christians. This can be verified by the fact that various denominations within Christianity (i.e., the different types of Christian churches—Baptist, Methodist, Pentecostal,

Presbyterian, etc. (there are a lot more than these)–all agree to the fact that God is a triune God. Even Christian churches that do not affiliate with a denomination believe in a triune God. There may be differences in how each denomination goes about sharing what it knows, but those differences are not contradictory to (do not argue against) the basic principles of Christianity. Different denominations of Christian churches may do things different, but their basic theology is the same.

Misnomers About God: Among Christians

Perhaps this basic principle discussion seems a little long-winded and preachy, but it is very important to have a basic understanding of God. I realized this more than ever after seeing teenager after teenager struggling with the question of whether or not they had obtained salvation (were saved) and if they could hang on to it. The Bible is very clear of the need for salvation, how to obtain it, and how it is maintained through a relationship with the triune God. Yet, there are differences of opinions as to what one will do or can do or must do when they have obtained salvation. This variance (difference) in opinion causes uncertainty in those who cannot determine which opinion is the most accurate. They cannot determine, because they have not developed a basic theology of God.

I noticed for a certain period of time that several teenagers were not participating in church activities (choir, youth Bible study, communion, etc.) because they were not sure if they were saved yet or still. All the opinions on what they will, can, and must do to be saved had them confused quite a bit. When they were asked, "Are you saved?" some would respond with the adolescent standard: "I don't know."

Now, some of the kids knew they had something they needed to fix in the relationship between them and God or someone else. Because they had not fixed this problem, they chose not to participate in communion. They did the right thing in waiting. 1 Corinthians 11:28 tells us to check our relationships and make sure they are in good standing before we participate in communion. So, concerning communion, they were obeying what they knew from Scripture. In other activities, however, they were just confused in where they stood in their relationship with God.

Generally their reason for the uncertainty was they didn't really understand what being saved meant and what it required of them. For that reason, they would say, "I don't know." In some cases, they had done something against God's will. In other cases, it was just against other folks' wills (such as church folks, folks at home or just folks in general). They were getting information on determining God's will from folks who didn't really know God. If a person doesn't know God's Word, then they don't know God and they don't know God's will.

Those kids still had some desire to sin at times or were not meeting the requirements of the opinionated (those who think they know it all). They felt they must not be saved because of that. The uncertainty of what it takes to be saved left those kids wondering if they were saved or even could obtain salvation.

This type of uncertainty or doubt has a very detrimental (damaging) effect on our relationship with God. We've already seen that without faith in God it is impossible to please God. Doubting Jesus' life was enough to remove one's debt to sin simply cannot be pleasing to God. So, what does that do to the relationship? It works against it. It replaces our faith, which we *should* have with fear, which we *should not* have. We need to take a close look at the effects of this fear. We'll get back to the subject of a simple theology in a little bit, but we really need to address this fear thing.

The scripture we'll be working with is 2 Timothy 1:7, "For God hath not given us the spirit of fear; but of power, and of love, and of a sound mind (KJV)." With study of Scripture, we always need to read verses around any single verse we want to understand to make sure we keep it in the right perspective. It's called capturing the background to stay within the context. The background scriptures are 2 Timothy 1:6 and 8-12. It's a little long; but hang in there with me. Grab a Coke® or Mountain Dew® or something. Do the Dew. Here are the Scriptures:

⁶Wherefore I put thee in remembrance that thou stir up the gift of God, which is in thee by the putting on of my hands. ⁷For God hath not given us the spirit of fear; but of power, and of love, and of a sound mind. ⁸Be not thou therefore ashamed of the testimony of our Lord, nor of me his prisoner, but be thou partaker of the

afflictions of the gospel according to the power of God; [9]Who hath saved us, and called us with an holy calling, not according to our works, but according to his own purpose and grace, which was given us in Christ Jesus before the world began, [10]But is now made manifest by the appearing of our Saviour Jesus Christ, who hath abolished death, and hath brought life and immortality to light through the gospel. [11]Whereunto I am appointed a preacher, and an apostle, and a teacher of the Gentiles. [12]For the which cause I also suffer these things. nevertheless I am not ashamed. For I know whom I have believed, and am persuaded that he is able to keep that which I have committed unto him against that day (KJV).

I once had a discussion with a young preacher (we'll call them Y.P.) on what keeps Christians saved or what keeps them from committing sin. This conversation was sparked by the fact that some believe once a person is saved they are always saved, but others believe if a person is not careful, they can lose their salvation after they receive it. This is really a hot topic for theological debaters and it seems to be an unsolvable equation. If the argument is that one is always saved, then the counterargument is people can sin as much as they want and still have a meaningful relationship with God. That is not so. If the argument is one can lose their salvation, then the counterargument is what Christ did on the cross to save us or His offer of the Holy Spirit to keep us was not enough. That is not so. The discussion can get really deep after that point, if you want it to.

However, there's no need for us to get deep and theoretical or enter into a theological debate about this. We just need to examine Scriptures and go with what is found there (stick with the recipe). In fact, that is the case with any debate on Biblical theory. Our theories on the Bible and Biblical truth might not always align with each other. People can say, "I think," "I believe," or "It should be understood" as much as they want when talking about Scripture. That does not make what they are saying Biblical truth, though. Biblical truth is what the Bible says–nothing else. The way we understand Biblical truth is by careful examination of Biblical text; or staying with the recipe as I have stated over and over.

My take in this discussion with Y.P. was if we are confident in our salvation, it keeps us from wanting to commit sin. We should be confident in knowing God's love is so powerful it overcomes sin or better said–over*came* sin. Each time something goes wrong in our relationship with God, the devil would like to steal our faith, kill our commitment and destroy our hope in salvation. He would have us to think we are stuck in a perpetual (continuing) position of separation from God. But Jesus took us out of that position, remember? He declared in John 10:10, "The thief comes only to steal and kill and destroy; I came that they may have life, and have it abundantly."

So, God has covered what sin had done to humankind. Once someone accepts God's offering of grace, they are under His covering and sin does not have the effect on them it once did–always hovering over them; always controlling them, keeping them separated from God.

They are hopeful from that point on in a confident hope, not an *iffy* hope. They do not know exactly how they will conduct themselves at any given moment, but they know they are becoming more and more like Christ. They know one day they will become like Him. That is from a human standpoint. I'm not saying they will become gods or another Christ. They will have all His good humanly characteristics all the time–one day. We might not have it quite together now, but one day... That is the point being made in 1 John 3:2-3. It says,

> ²Dear friends, now we are children of God, and what we will be has not yet been made known. But we know that when he [Christ] appears, we shall be like him, for we shall see him as he is. ³Everyone who has this hope in him purifies himself, just as he [Christ] is pure. (Brackets added for clarity.)

It is the purification which comes from having this hope in God's ability to cover our sin, that keeps us from wanting to sin. In verses 6, 8, and 9 of 1 John 3, it explains if people are in this position of hope (abiding under God's covering), then they have no desire to sin against Him, but if they are not in that position of hope (still under the control of sin) then they still desire to sin.

The word for sin in each of those verses is hamartano and it means to 'wander from the law.' So, this is not a single act of sin as if you or I did something wrong out of impulse or in a moment of weakness or purely by accident. No, the sin described here is turning away from God and having a desire to sin on a regular basis and no more desire to do God's will. If a person is under God's covering, if they have salvation, they will not just want to wander away from doing right (according to what God's word says is right). The person's confidence in God keeps them from intentionally sinning; even if they mistakenly do something wrong; or in a moment of weakness do something wrong; or get tricked into doing something wrong.

Their desire is to do right. From a human perspective, our desire drives what we will want to do and not want to do. If we desire to serve God, then our desire will be to not sin against Him. So, we won't intentionally do so. If, we unintentionally sin against Him, we will feel sorry, we will correct our actions and we will try our best not to repeat those actions. We never stop loving God and He never stops loving us during this process. The process is called repentance. We are human. We will occasionally mess up. Paul explains this well in Romans 7:14-25. He talks about a constant struggle against sin. Even though we try hard, we still sometimes fall short. Nonetheless, what Christ did on our behalf still gives us the victory over it all.

If we study the life of King David in the Old Testament, we can see this process in action. The Bible exemplifies (demonstrates) that nobody loved God like David did. It also shows God loved and blessed David. The Bible also gives accounts of David's serious mistakes–sins against God. It shows, in spite of those mistakes, David's love for God did not waiver, nor did God's love for David.

Acts 10:34 tells us God is not a respecter of persons. God loves us when we make mistakes just as much as He loved King David when he made mistakes. Our mistakes should lessen as we grow closer to God, but we will still make them until we become like Christ. 1 John 2:1-2 tells us, "My little children, I am writing these things to you so that you may not sin. And if anyone sins, we have an Advocate with the Father, Jesus Christ the righteous; and He Himself is the propitiation for our sins; and not for ours only, but also for those of the whole world." It is obvious that we will make mistakes, even after we've obtained salvation. You should never believe anyone who tells you that you are not saved if you have sinned after you accept Christ as Lord. However, don't take that knowledge as an excuse to sin. We have no excuse for sinning. John starts verse 1 above with stating that he's giving us information from God which will keep us from wanting to sin. We should be growing further away from sinful mistakes or sinful desires and closer to sinless-ness in Jesus Christ.

Y.P.'s presumption (opinion) was it is a person's fear of going to hell that keeps them from sinning. In fact, they said concerning their grandmother, "My grandmother did not fear hell, because she knew she was saved, but I am saved, because I fear hell." That seemed like a pretty deep statement for such a young preacher–still in their teens. It sounded very philosophical. For a minute, you'd think, "Wow!"

But after getting over the awe of Y.P.'s poetic proclamation you have to think, "So, folks keep from sinning, because they're afraid of losing their salvation." Well, this statement should lead the Christian straight to the message in 2 Timothy 1:7. "For God hath not given us the spirit of fear; but of power, and of love, and of a sound mind (KJV)." There is a clear contradiction there, isn't it? The Law of Non-Contradiction has been broken. Now, we as Christians have no choice but to say, "That's the wrong formula. That doesn't line up with the truth of Scripture. It's not true."

It has been said that a certain amount of fear is healthy for a person. There is some truth to that. This is evident by observing someone in fear. If a person who fears heights gets close to a very steep, very high cliff, they will fear falling off. That fear will keep them from getting too close to the edge, so that is a good thing, right? I think so. I hope you do, too, if you hang around cliffs!

Well, that fear is an emotion. However, the same person that once feared falling off of cliffs might one day repel from them (slide down the side) on a rope. I did–when I was in the Army–from high walls, cliffs and even helicopters in mid air. The first time was petrifying (I was nearly scared to death). Of course, trying to be a hero, I hid my fear. After a few times; it was actually a lot of fun. By the third or fourth trip, I was yelling like a kid going down that cliff, "Woo Hoooo!!!" That was fun! Why the change in my attitude toward steep cliffs and other high places? It is because this fear was just an emotion. We can overcome our emotions.

But that's the emotion of fear. The fear in the aforementioned text (2 Timothy 1:7) is not an emotion. It is a spirit. We want to overcome some of our emotions. Some spirits want to overcome us. This is exemplified (demonstrated) throughout the Bible where some people overcame their emotions by the Spirit of God, but others' emotions are controlled by evil spirits. Look at the story of Moses. He was emotionally afraid of going to Pharaoh and speaking against him, but the Spirit of God gave him the strength to overcome his emotions and do it. On the other hand, in the passage of Scripture at Mark 5:1-5 and Luke 8:26-29, we see an example of a man being controlled by evil spirits. We try to control our emotions. Spirits try to control us. That's why 1 John 4:1 tells us to test spirits to make sure they are from God.

We don't have to question whether the spirit of fear is an evil spirit. The text in 2 Timothy 1:7 points out that "the spirit of fear" is not a spirit from God. And if it is not from God it must be from the devil, making it an evil spirit. So, the devil brought this spirit onto the scene. In fact, we can just about pinpoint when he did it if we read Genesis 3:10 closely. This verse gives the first account of an incident in which humankind was controlled by the spirit of fear.

Let's go back to the emotion of fear for now. We can overcome the emotion of fear. When a baby first learns to walk, somebody has to entice him or her to let go of whatever they are holding on to and take those first few clumsy steps. This is because the baby fears falling. They have fallen a time or two, and they have realized through the baby philosophical process that falling is not fun. It hurts. So, they are afraid to fall anymore.

Parents and older relatives will do all they can to get that baby to overcome this fear of falling. They will use crazy voices—"Come on. Come to papa. Come to mama. You can do it." They will use shiny, noisy or colorful objects. They may use the baby's bottle or Scooby Snacks—okay just snacks. They will use all sorts of tricks to get that baby to let go. What they are doing is stirring up the baby's emotion of excitement, trying to help them overcome their emotion of fear. Eventually, they will succeed in doing so. I have never heard of a case where someone has failed in convincing a baby you don't have to be scared of falling when you walk. The baby's emotion of excitement always overcomes their emotion of fear. So, the baby takes a couple of steps—then a couple more. Soon they are running through the house, even though they're told not to. They have overcome the emotional fear of falling.

You see what I mean? The emotion of fear can be overcome. A person's emotion of excitement can overcome the emotion of fear every time. You ever watch extreme sports on TV? Those folks do a lot of crazy stunts. Some of that stuff I wouldn't think about doing. Do you ever wonder if they weren't scared the first few times? The emotion of fear does not stop them, because the emotion of excitement from which comes the enjoyment of doing those extreme sports just overcomes that fear. Fear doesn't stop them.

In the same manner, the emotion of fear will not stop a person (at least not for long) from desiring to sin as suggested by Y.P. That's because of the emotion of excitement in committing some of those sins. (Yeah, we know that some sins can be very exciting.) That excitement will overcome their fear quickly. Fear doesn't stop them.

Again, that is emotional fear. We can control our emotion of fear. Spiritual fear wants to control us. Since this spirit is not from God (the text states that), then, it is a spirit from the devil which tries to control people. Contrary (opposite), then, to Y.P.'s philosophical sounding statement, fear does not push a person toward God. It pulls a person away from God. The spirit of fear is the reason people do not seek a better relationship with God once they come to know about Him.

For a Biblical example, let's go back to the discussion on the first occurrence of fear. Gen 3:10 gives us the account of Adam's response as to why he hid himself from God. "He [Adam] said, 'I heard the sound of You in the garden, and I was *afraid* because I was naked; so I hid myself.'" (Brackets and emphasis added.)

Now, Adam already had a perfect knowledge of God's love. He had enjoyed a beautiful relationship with God. His needs had always been completely fulfilled by God. He had always been able to openly talk to God. They had an absolutely flawless companionship. His love for and faith in God were perfectly placed. So, Adam had no reason to have an emotional fear of God.

Yet, with Adam's first encounter with the devil and with the perpetration (introduction) of sin, the devil slipped in a spirit that would cause Adam to want to separate or hide from God rather than take advantage of the wonderful relationship God had for him. The faith Adam once had in God was now a fear of God. Sin had changed the relationship humankind had with God, and fear was the first indication that the relationship had changed from what it was before sin. Y.P's philosophy suddenly begins to lose its luster, doesn't it? It no longer seems to be brilliant thinking.

Youth have often said they're afraid they are not ready yet for salvation. I have heard some say they do not want to be saved yet, because they don't know if they can commit to being good all the time. Based on those statements the biggest reason, then, is the same reason Adam had from the beginning. They are afraid God will see them exposed (as they really are) and will not accept them. Adam was naked and felt like he was in no condition to come before God. Those youth feel, like Adam did, that they are in no condition to come before God. So, they hide in fear.

There are several reasons for waiting to be saved (or not accepting God's salvation yet) even when we understand the benefits and the need of salvation. However, all those reasons are driven by the spirit of fear. Fear has no place in God's plan of salvation. In fact, fear is an indication one has not fully developed a loving relationship with God. Here is what 1 John 4:18 says concerning fear and God's love: "There is no fear in love; but perfect love casts out fear, because fear involves punishment, and the one who fears is not perfected in love." You should read that fourth chapter of 1 John when you have a chance. It really helps us know that the spirit of fear as well as other spirits that are not of God can hinder our relationship with Him. It also shows us how God builds relationships on love and not fear.

So, rather than push people closer to God (as Y.P. suggested), the spirit of fear tries to separate people from God. Fear is the enemy of faith. That is why God gave something that will win out over the spirit of fear, which is seen in 2 Timothy 1:7: power, love, and a sound mind. Again, it reads, "For God hath not given us the spirit of fear, but of power and of love and of a sound mind (KJV)."

The Greek word for power as it is used here is *dunamis*. It means ability. We don't need to study Greek to know what Paul meant here by love. The Greek word for sound mind (the two words make up a compound word) is *sophronismos*. It means self-control.

So, after a little diligent word study, we see what Paul is saying here a little clearer. Rather than leaving us with the fear of whether or not we can make this Christian walk (live a saved lifestyle or Christ-like life), God has given us the *ability* through His *love* to *control* (discipline) our*selves* for this Christian journey. It can be done and if we focus on this thought, it will be done. This is important for us Christians to know—especially the young Christians or 'young in faith' Christians.

Fear seems to be the biggest setback for Christians who don't walk in their faith. They have fear of not being good enough. They have fear of not being acceptable. They have fear of not knowing exactly what is required of us. They just have too much fear. Paul looked to squash that fear, so that young and new Christians can live a victorious life in Christ Jesus.

In verse 6, Paul tells young Timothy to stir up the gift. Some of you may have read this before and thought about the gifts God has given the church for ministry, but that is not what this gift is. If you notice, it is a singular gift, not plural like those spiritual gifts. The Greek word for gift as it is used here is *charisma*. Sounds familiar, doesn't it? The English word charisma means "a special magnetic charm." In the ancient Greek culture (as it is used in this passage) it meant that divine grace which leads to eternal salvation. The two meanings sound pretty close, don't they; magnetic; being lead to or drawn to? This Greek *charisma* is the gift of salvation God uses to draw us back to a good relationship with Him. Don't we just love to be around charismatic people? They just draw us to them, because they're such a joy to be around. Well, nobody does charisma like God.

The Greek word for stir up used here is *anazopureo*. It means inflame one's mind; have some zeal (excitement) about this thing. That's the excitement we need to overcome the fear. Only this time it's spiritual excitement to overcome spiritual fear rather than emotional excitement to overcome emotional fear. So, Paul is saying our minds ought to be excited about our salvation. Spiritual excitement is an excellent repellant for spiritual fear.

In verse 8 Paul says do not be ashamed of a testimony. A testimony is the story of receiving our salvation. It is how God delivered this gift to us. Receiving gifts is always exciting. It's even more exciting to show off and tell others about your gift. How many times have you been excited about getting to school the next day to show off the new pair of shoes your parents bought for you? If you are excited about your salvation, then you will be excited about sharing that, too, and not ashamed of letting others know you have received it.

In verse 10 Paul lets us know this gift was made possible through Jesus' resurrection. If you pay close attention, you should see where Paul said it was manifested (made known) through Jesus' appearance who hath (that's past tense) abolished death. What needed to be done to make salvation possible has already been done. There is nothing more you can do to obtain salvation, except receive it. You only need to accept it as a gift from God.

In verse 11 Paul shows how the gift can be received. We receive this gift through hearing and accepting it from those whom God has appointed to preach and teach it. As we discussed previously, faith comes by hearing the Word of God. Hearing, in this case, means to be taught.

Finally, in verse 12 Paul lets us know God will not let us slip away once we have heard and *accepted* this gospel. Paul was confident of that. Why was Paul so confident? He was confident because Jesus, Himself, said He will not lose any that belong to Him. John 10:27-29 records these words.

[27]My [this is Jesus talking] sheep hear my voice, and I know them, and they follow me [we hear the gospel, we accept the gospel, we become His followers–i.e., Christians]. [28]And I give unto them eternal life [salvation]; and they shall never perish, neither shall any man pluck them out of my hand. [29]My Father, which gave them me, is greater than all; and no man is able to pluck them out of my Father's hand. (Brackets added for clarification.)

Paul shows the same confidence in Christ in 2 Timothy 1:12 stating, "…for I know whom I have believed and I am convinced that He is able to guard what I have entrusted to Him until that day." The writer of the book of Hebrews writes in Hebrews 7:25 concerning Jesus Christ, "Therefore He is able also to save forever those who draw near to God through Him, since He always lives to make intercession for them."

We as Christians today should have the same faith (confidence) in Jesus' words as did Paul. And if we have faith, we will not have fear. God's gift to us is not fear. It is power, love and a sound mind. It is the ability, by God's gift of love, to have self-discipline. We should not allow the spirit of fear to have any control in us; causing us to worry if we are saved or when we are going to do something to cost us our salvation. We ought to use self-control (or self-discipline) with the ability God has lovingly given us and have no doubts of where our salvation lies. We ought to rejoice and be confident in God's gift. That's enough to keep us from wanting to sin.

Okay, now getting back to the topic of simple theology. Where does all this discussion fit? The simple theology of a triune God can remove a lot of doubt and clear you to have a good relationship with God. That relationship will grow and equip you to move away from a sinful lifestyle and into a better relationship with God. A godly (Christian) lifestyle will accompany that relationship. The basic knowledge that God is a loving Father, God is a forgiving Savior and God is a helping Spirit can move this relationship along.

The Christian's relationship with God is made complete because of God's triune nature. Humankind began with a wonderful relationship with God the Father, but forfeited (gave up) that relationship by sinning against Him. The departure from the Father's presence left us condemned to the effects of sin. We were at sin's mercy or I should say–sin's *lack of* mercy. God the Father loved us so much He sent His Son to remove the condemning power of sin. Upon receiving God the Son as Savior, we no longer have to be subjected to the condemning effects of sin. We can once again enjoy a wonderful relationship with God the Father. God the Holy Spirit gives us the knowledge and the power we need to continue in this new relationship with God the Father much like the relationship before humankind sinned. This is the most basic theology (or knowledge) of God. We can see that it is important to have a good knowledge of who God is. It is important to have a good basic theology.

If many of the teenagers I mentioned before had a good knowledge of God, then they would have a clear understanding of why they need to be saved, what they must do to get saved, and how they maintain salvation. There'd be no more, "I don't know" (or lack of faith). They'd no longer have to wonder if they're saved when they don't measure up to others' expectations. They could see that anything beyond the Bible requirements for salvation is just extra-curricular activity. That activity is not always bad; it may just be how a certain person or group or church goes about acknowledging or demonstrating their love for God. So it may not be a bad thing, but any change in God's plan for salvation is bad. The extra-curricular activity we take part in is done to show our affection and reverence (respect) for God. It is *not* a requirement for salvation. We should always be sure we do not feel it is something we must do to obtain or retain salvation. Every person needs salvation. All salvation needs is a belief (faith) in Jesus as Lord and sincere commitment to Him. The Holy Spirit will help those who obtain salvation to keep that commitment.

Among Non-Christians

Again, there are some religions which claim Christianity as their base, but do not recognize the triune person of God. They do not follow the basic formula for Christianity. Well, the first principle of logic still applies. You can't start with the truth, veer (turn) from it and continue to call it truth. The law of non-contradiction also applies here. You can't call yourself a Christian and be in clear disagreement with basic Christian principles. Likewise, the idea of changing the formula for water still applies in this case. If you change anything in the elemental makeup (the formula–in this case what Christ provided as truth), you have a totally different substance (in this case a different belief system). That belief system is no longer Christianity. It no longer has Christianity as its basic principle. In cases where people incorporate those changes, they falsely identify themselves as Christians. This causes a great deal of confusion for those outside of Christianity. It appears to outsiders that Christianity holds to opposing truths (has different beliefs) within its body of believers (as Person2 misunderstood). This is not the case.

Since we're on the subject, let me reiterate Person2's other misunderstanding. They expressed that Christians will have no real relationships outside of their own circle. We must hold very close to Biblical truth and demonstrate this in our interactions with others. In other words, we must really live a Christ-like life if we say we are Christians. Living Christ-like does not make it impossible or even difficult for us to live in harmony with those around us who do not hold to our values. In fact, the opposite is true. The principles of Christianity help us as believers live in harmony with non-believers.

I suppose most of us have very close friends who do not accept the truth of Christianity. I do and I feel certain you do as well. I even have some family members that I simply adore who choose not to believe Biblical facts demonstrated through Christianity. I don't doubt you do, too. Yet, we Christians still hold those friendships and relationships in the highest regards. I can't count the times I've spoken with Christians who are deeply concerned about their friends and loved ones who do not believe or follow Christian doctrine. They show concern for their overall well-being, both physical and spiritual. So, Person2's claim that we as Christians choose to alienate (isolate) ourselves, because of our desire to stay with the Bible's original formula for Christianity is way off the mark.

Conclusion

Knowing exactly who God is plays a huge part in our relationship with Him (and with others). Knowledge of God is crucial if we are to love Him and others. In Paul's letter to the church at Philippi, he prayed they would grow in knowledge and discernment (insight). He said doing so would make their desire to love God sincere and would keep them from offending one another. It reads in Philippians 1:9-10,

And this I pray, that your love may abound yet more and more in knowledge and judgment [discernment]; that ye may approve the things that are excellent; that ye may be sincere and without offence till the day of Christ. (KJV–Brackets added for clarity.)

This is why theology is important to us. It does not have to be a theology that answers every question about God. We don't have to go that deep. We can't go that deep. No one will be able to determine everything about God in this life. The Bible states that in 1 Corinthians 13:12. It says that now we see things only in part and not totally clear, but in the end we will see everything as it really is. Read it when you have a moment. You should have a moment now.

We should admire those people who know most of the facts of Biblical history. I sure do. We should also admire those who can bring out Biblical principles in a way that can be easily understood even in today's changing culture—like some of the great preachers and teachers we know. Only the basics are totally necessary, however, to begin and maintain a good relationship with God. The rest will come in due time.

Knowing the basics gives a person what they need for a meaningful relationship with God. If that person accepts the difficult-to-understand triune person of God, then they have the basics for knowing a Father who loves them, a Son who saves them, and a Spirit who keeps them. Prepared with this information, they can begin to give an answer for why they believe what they believe. The answer becomes more complete as they study God's Word and build this relationship they have with Him through his Son, Jesus Christ, with the help of the Holy Spirit. Theology (knowledge of God) helps us to know this and it helps us share this with others, which brings up our next subject: sharing the knowledge of God.

3 SHARING THE KNOWLEDGE OF GOD

Not sharing the faith is like not sharing the cure (Rf. Proverbs 4:20-22)

The Joy of Sharing

This chapter discusses evangelism as the key component in the Christian faith. It examines the importance of evangelism from two viewpoints: why evangelism is so extremely necessary and how to accomplish effective evangelism. There is no benefit to having useful knowledge if we don't share it, right? The intent here is not to build a case for evangelism; the case has already been built, torn down and rebuilt (all in three days). The intent here is to rekindle the fire every born-again Christian believer has once had for spreading the Good News, which is the Gospel of Jesus Christ. The intent is to invoke (stir up) a renewed desire to evangelize–a desire that is fueled by faith.

If you believe what you know is true, you should be absolutely thrilled to share that truth. Paul E. Little declares in his book, *How to Give Away Your Faith*, that "Faith is the key to maintaining the reality of our Christian experience."[1] If we Christians know our faith to be real, then we should share our Christian experience (by some means– conversation, actions, or reactions) among everyone with whom we come in contact.

If someone knew the cure for cancer, that would be a remarkable thing. If they chose not to share it, that would be a horrible thing. In fact, most people would consider that person heartless. If Christians never share their knowledge of God (the cure to the eternal illness of sin) with those who have not yet found that cure, it would be just as horrible. The sharing of that knowledge of God (as you are most likely aware) is called evangelism.

Although there are many elements which make up the overall composition of the Christian faith, evangelism is one of the most important elements. Evangelism is the lifeblood that allows Christianity to continue to exist. It is to the Christian faith what the Energizer® battery is to the Energizer® Bunny–it keeps it going and going. Every Christian must certainly know Jesus Christ is the source of this lifeblood, so unlike batteries, there is unlimited power. Mr. E. Bunny won't last forever; God's Word will, though.

Of course, this chapter is not designed to make you think that if you don't share the Gospel, then it won't get shared. The Gospel (the message that Jesus Christ is Lord) will go forth. Jesus lets us know this when he responded to the religious leaders who asked Him to make the people stop calling him Lord. Jesus told them that if the people stopped proclaiming Him as Lord, then the rocks will cry it out (cf. Luke 19:37-40). So, the message will go forth with us or without us. It is not necessary that we be the ones to spread the good news. It's just natural for us to want to spread it, and it is a privilege to do so.

This natural desire to proclaim Christ to people (or evangelize) resides in every Christian. Our desire to share our faith in the Gospel of Jesus Christ with others comes naturally. It's like when something really exciting happens to you and all you want to do is share it. It compares to when a little kid comes home with an all 'A' report card.

They don't wait for Mom or Dad to ask if teachers sent reports cards for that period. They have it in their hand when they climb into the car or enter the front door; clearly visible.

Then again, maybe it's more like when a kid wins first place in some competition and their parents were not there when the competition took place. So, they come up to the car or into the house with their trophy or ribbon in plain view to make sure the entire household knows they have accomplished something great. That's what the desire to evangelize is like. You just want everybody to know about your acceptance of salvation.

Maybe you recall first being saved (receiving Christ's salvation). Well, that feeling of joy you were eager to share is the purest form of a desire to evangelize others. That is when you wanted nothing more than for everyone around you to experience what you had just gone through. You wanted to tell the good news: you are now a Christian. That is a natural instinct for Christians. We want to be evangelists.

We should not be afraid of or uncomfortable with being called an 'evangelist.' You are probably familiar with the term as a title for those in the ministry who have been ordained (confirmed) as such. Yes, there is the title of Evangelist (notice the uppercase 'E' depicting a proper noun) for those who are ordained to go out and perform a specific task for the church. However, the word evangelist–lowercase 'e'–(*euaggelistes* in Greek) simply means "a bringer of good tidings." 'Tidings' is just another word for news. All Christians are commissioned (authorized, appointed, charged) by Jesus Christ to bring the Good News to folks.

For the record, there is also a title for ministers who are ordained to serve a specific task within the church. Every Christian, however, plays a part in service to Christ and to others, so that makes all Christians ministers as well. The Greek word for minister (*diakoneo*) means to serve. The common evangelist is just one who shares the Good News of Jesus to others, just as the common minister is one who serves Christ and others.

You might think since evangelism is such a key component to the Christian faith, that it should receive more concentration of effort from Christians than any other Christian activity. This is based on the fact that Christians should realize this is what will further the knowledge of God throughout the world. Evangelism should be the first priority of each Christian individual, group, church, and organization in the world. That does not seem to be the case though.

Evangelism's Origin: From the Foundation

To understand evangelism's origin, you must really understand the meaning of evangelism. The original Greek meaning was given, but we may need a little more discussion on the subject. Different authors and theologians offer their definitions for what it means to evangelize. Although all the definitions are similar, some carry more completeness in their meaning than others.

In his book, *Handbook for Youth Evangelism*, Dean Finley defines evangelism as "the processes, procedures, and activities of any Christian sharing the Gospel with a non-Christian".[2] George Barna does not give an 'official' definition of evangelism in his book, *Evangelism That Works*, but he does partly describe it as "the act of sharing your faith with a non-believer".[3] Of course, the Merriam-Webster definition should be included, since English-speaking folks base most of their understanding of an English word on what Merriam-Webster offers. Merriam-Webster defines evangelism as, "the winning or revival [renewal] of personal commitments to Christ."[4] (Brackets added.) I didn't expect *that* from Merriam-Webster, but I sure did like it!

As you can see, the different definitions take different approaches to arriving at similar conclusive meanings. (They all go at it a different way, but say pretty much the same thing.) Each, however, has varying degrees of completeness. They all are true, but they are not all complete. Perhaps one of the most complete definitions of evangelism I have ever seen is one offered by Dr. David Kitchens, a professor at Luther Rice University in Lithonia, Georgia (Metro Atlanta) in one of his weekly lectures. Dr. Kitchen's definition of evangelism is:

God intervening in the affairs of man [humankind] through submissive vessels, seeking that men [humankind] will hear, respond, submit, repent and serve the proclaimed Lord of the universe, Jesus Christ.[5] (Brackets added.)

Yeah, he gets a little deep with it, but that's what seminary professors do. His definition is really quite simple, though, when you think about it. In Dr. Kitchen's definition, we can identify God the Father as the One who causes evangelism to happen, Jesus Christ the Son as the subject of that evangelism, and humankind as recipient and distributor of the Good News about Jesus Christ.

We also see (after close examination) that evangelism is founded upon the idea of God desiring an up close and personal relationship with every person. He offers that relationship through His Son, Jesus Christ. So our goal as evangelists for Christ, then, is to initiate the relationship between Him and others. Reaching that goal involves (in accordance with Dr. Kitchen's definition) a five-step process:

- Present the invitation from God to others
- Get them to respond to that invitation
- Get them to submit to (or accept) that invitation
- Get them to repent (or end their relationship with ungodliness)
- Get them to build their relationship with God and present God's invitation to others

God sends His invitation by way of those who have already received and accepted it. That's us—those who have already obtained salvation. It's sort of like an invitation to a party for a new kid in the neighborhood. A parent wants to throw a party for their son to help him make new friends. The parents make out the invitations, pass them to a few kids who already know their son, and ask them to pass the invitations around to their friends and those they come in contact with.

It looks like it's going to be a really nice party, so the kids are all excited about spreading the word–passing out the invitations. Pretty soon kids all over are coming to the party and everybody just has a great time. That's what evangelism is like. It kind of reminds me of a song we old folks in the church sing: "When all of God's children get together–what a time!"

To the Founder

Jesus Christ is the founder of evangelism. He founded evangelism by sending out messengers with invitations to anyone who would accept. Matthew 28:19-20 ('the Great Commission' mentioned in chapter one) states Jesus instructed his disciples to:

[19]Go therefore and make disciples of all the nations, baptizing them in the name of the Father and the Son and the Holy Spirit, [20]teaching them to observe all that I commanded you; and lo, I am with you always, even to the end of the age.

This passage of Scripture records the founding of evangelism. Some people might contest (argue) that this commission was directed at Jesus' original disciples and not Christians living today. Well, Merriam-Webster defines a disciple as "one who accepts and helps to spread the teachings of another".[6] The Greek meaning of disciple, consequently, is essentially the same: *matheteuo*–to follow someone's precepts and instruction. Anyone who accepts Christ as their Savior and follows His teachings has become His disciple. Therefore, it is perfectly correct to say that anyone who accepts Jesus Christ as their Savior has been commissioned by Him to spread His gospel. In other words, all Christians are instructed to be evangelists.

The Reason Behind It All: A World Awry

So why should we evangelize? Have you ever heard the phrase, "What is this world coming to?" I feel fairly certain you've heard it. It is quoted so often that as soon as you hear it you immediately think about the sad condition of the world today. Just check the news on television, on radio, in the newspaper or even by word of mouth for a few minutes. I know. I'm preaching again; but just do it for a few minutes. You will get a full dose of murder, rape, robbery and countless other crimes reported throughout the world.

All types of people are committing these crimes from heads of nations to those who are considered least among citizens. These crimes don't just happen on an individual basis. Individuals commit crimes against groups. Groups commit crimes against other groups. Crimes are even being committed against entire countries.

The Bible states in Proverbs 14:12 and 16:25 (This was so important it was repeated), "There is a way which seems right to a man, but its end is the way of death." These crimes take place so often because people have developed such a tolerance for sin (sin does not bother them anymore). To some it seems like sin is the only way. In some cases they even think it's the right way. For some, even killing seems the right way. They kill to solve problems. They kill to gain power. Sometimes it seems they kill for no apparent reason at all.

R. J. Rummel, Professor Emeritus (retired, but still actively involved) of political science at the University of Hawaii, coined the term (made up the word) democide. It means:

The murder of any person or people by a government, including genocide [the deliberate and systematic destruction of a racial, political, or cultural group], politicide [the same as genocide, but strictly for political reasons], and mass murder [murdering a large number of people, typically at the same time or over a relatively short period of time][7] (Brackets added for clarity.)

According to Rummel's research paper, *Statistics of Democide*, posted on the *www.hawaii.edu/powerkills* website, "the overall democide for the [time period of] 1928-1987 [is] 76,702,000."[8] (Brackets Added.) That means governments legally (according to their own law) killed over seventy-six million people in less than sixty years. They felt it was the right thing to do. If they knew and accepted the love of God and understood the love he wants us to have for each other, there's no way they could agree to such senseless killing of so many people.

This statistic gives a vivid (clear) picture of the condition of the world today and how valid (true) the Word of God is in Proverbs 14:12. They think they are doing something right, but it's ending up in death—a lot of deaths. This statistic gives the understanding of why there is an urgent need for evangelism in today's world. The Word of God is not known or understood by many people in this world;

therefore, their ways are not God's ways. Some people have a very bad idea of what is the right thing to do.

The best way to change their mindset is to make them aware of God's love through the practice of evangelism. According to 2 Peter 3:9,

> The Lord is not slack concerning his promise, as some men count slackness; but is longsuffering to us-ward, not willing that any should perish, but that all should come to repentance.

Simply stated, this passage says God's will for humankind is that none of them perish (die). Evangelism is the perfect way to inform the world that God did not plan for so many to die from democidal causes.

A Nation in Need

The number stated above for democidal death worldwide is astronomical (really big). Americans do not have to travel the entire globe, however, to realize the effects of sin on the world today. This nation, our United States of America, has enough of its own woes (troubles) to necessitate (call for) an increase in evangelism.

There is definitely a need for evangelism in our country. Jesus is recorded in Matt 9:37 as saying, "The harvest truly is plenteous, but the labourers are few." He is saying there are a lot of people that need to be reached through evangelism and not enough of us are reaching them. According to George Barna's research results, the following was true in 1995:

> There are 320,000 Protestant [Christian churches that are not Catholic] and Catholic churches in the United States. There are probably 800,000 ordained or full-time, church-based ministers. There are about 50,000 missionaries. There are an estimated 2,000,000 to 3,000,000 people who possess the gift of evangelism.[9]

The gift of evangelism means they are really good at sharing the Gospel. Even with the huge number of avenues through which the Gospel could travel, Barna suggests that 187,000,000 of the 262,000,000 Americans in 1995 had not accepted Jesus Christ as their Lord and Savior. That is over seventy-one percent. That's a plenteous harvest. With such a huge percentage of the population unsaved, we can see the urgent need of evangelism in our country.

A Choking Church

If we continue to drill down and search where the need for evangelism lies, we'd naturally consider the church as the next place to address. In the introduction to their book, *Power in the Pulpit*, Jerry Vines and Jim Shaddox begin with the following story:

> Upon meeting a fellow pastor who was studying his sermon notes, a well-meaning preacher declared, 'I don't study to preach. I just preach. I just get in the pulpit, and the Holy Spirit fills me.' The preacher who was studying his notes said, 'What if the Holy Spirit

doesn't fill you?' The other pastor replied, 'I just mess around until He does.' A lot of congregations would lament that too much messing around is going on and not enough preaching.[10]

There is evidence that evangelism is not happening enough in the one place we would expect it to–the church. As stated before, Barna claims nine out of ten American church goers can't accurately define the Great Commission found in Matthew 28:19-20 (we talked about it in chapter one). He says that seven out of ten have no clue what "John 3:16" talks about. We should definitely remember the words written in John 3:16, because they are a key element in basic evangelism.

Barna's research also shows that only thirty-one percent of American church folk can define "Gospel." Thus, the Gospel is clearly not being taught in some of our churches as it should be. If the Gospel is not being taught, then evangelism is not taking place, because evangelism involves spreading of the gospel. If evangelism is not taking place at the base station (in the church), then there is no wonder it is not being practiced (as much as it should be) outside of church. Because many church folks are not receiving the knowledge of God, they don't have the knowledge of God to share with others. You should evaluate the church you attend and make sure the gospel is being taught, so that you are being prepared to share it with others. If it isn't, you should be striving to stir up that gift in your church members.

Approaches to Evangelism: An Army of One

Evangelism can be achieved through many channels. Individuals certainly have been and continue to be a great source. Jesus told His disciples (as recorded in Matthew 10:7), "And as ye go, preach, saying, The kingdom of heaven is at hand." We've discussed the definition of disciple. Preach, in this case, just means to proclaim or tell. Every born-again believer should proclaim the gospel as they go about their daily business. Again, that proclamation does not always have to happen through spoken words. At some point the Word must be spoken, but actions play a huge part in evangelism as well.

In order to proclaim it, however, we must first learn it. Not only that, we must learn it correctly. The Apostle Paul says in 2 Tim 2:15, "Study to shew thyself approved unto God, a workman that needeth not to be ashamed, rightly dividing the word of truth (KJV)." Rightly dividing (*orthotomeo* in Greek) means to cut straight. We must use precision when sharing the Word of God.

Paul knew the importance of preparing before sharing. He left us with a directive to study before we begin to share God's Word. Therefore, each born-again believer should familiarize themselves with the scriptures and understand the meaning of scriptures. Having done so, they will be able to offer the gospel to others whenever the opportunity presents itself.

An excellent group of scriptures to learn and use for evangelism is a set of passages known as 'the Romans Road'. The Romans Road refers to passages of Scripture in the book of Romans which identify God's plan of salvation for humankind. Different teachers refer to different Scripture passages from the book of Romans when presenting the Romans Road, but the key passages consist of the following scriptures: Romans 3:23, 6:23, and 10:9. Romans 3:23 states: "For all have sinned, and come short of the glory of God." Romans 6:23 states, "For the wages of sin is death; but the gift of God is eternal life through Jesus Christ our Lord." Romans 10:9 states, "That if you confess with your mouth Jesus as Lord, and believe in your heart that God raised Him from the dead, you will be saved."

The version of the Romans Road presented in this book also includes passages of Scripture from Genesis 3:23 (to help explain the reason humankind needs to travel this road), Romans 5:8, Romans 5:12, and Romans 8:1. The Romans Road illustration is an excellent evangelism tool for you to use in directing someone to Jesus Christ; that is, once you have studied and understood the Scriptures enough to explain them. Here is an illustration of the Romans Road along with a full explanation of the Scriptures:

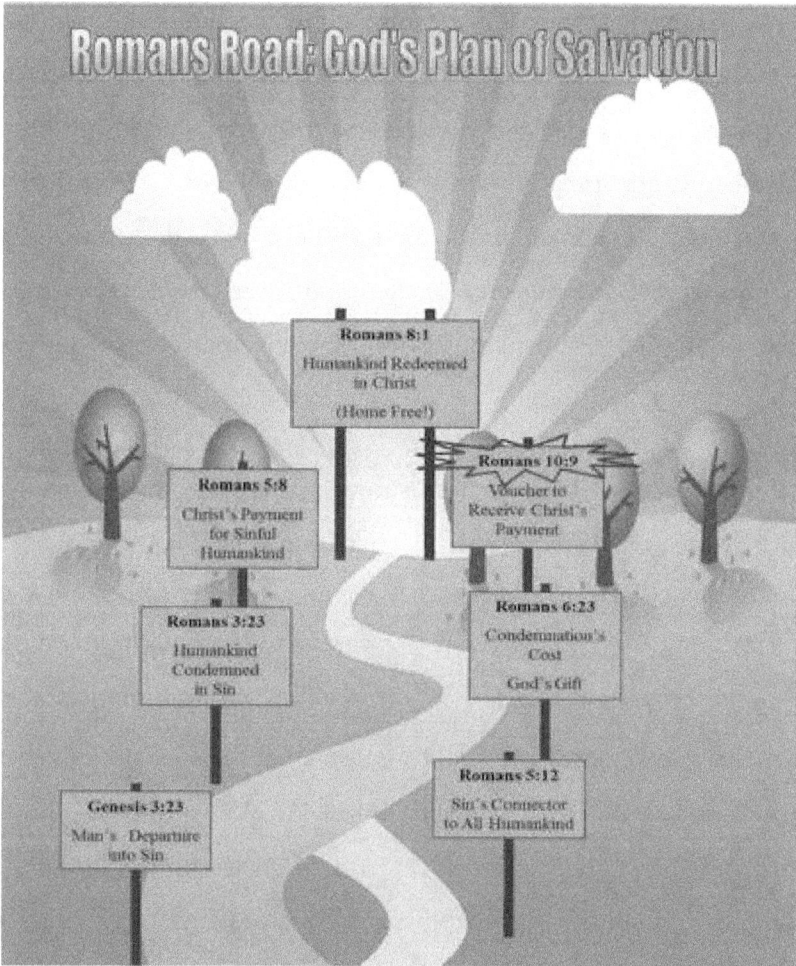

Romans Road: God's Plan of Salvation

Romans 8:1
Humankind Redeemed
in Christ
(Home Free!)

Romans 10:9
Voucher to
Receive Christ's
Payment

Romans 5:8
Christ's Payment
for Sinful
Humankind

Romans 3:23
Humankind
Condemned
in Sin

Romans 6:23
Condemnation's
Cost
God's Gift

Genesis 3:23
Man's Departure
into Sin

Romans 5:12
Sin's Connector
to All Humankind

The passage in Genesis 3:23 sums up the story of the first man's (Adam's) departure from a perfect relationship with God. It says, "Therefore the LORD God sent him out from the garden of Eden, to cultivate the ground from which he was taken." Man sinned against God and brought condemnation (guilt) on himself and all of humankind to follow. This left humankind under the conviction or power of sin. The entire story is recorded in the third chapter of Genesis.

The passage in Romans 5:12 explains how the nature of sin in Adam was passed to (or inherited by) all of humankind. It reads, "Therefore, just as through one man sin entered into the world, and death through sin, and so death spread to all men, because all sinned." This brought about a need for humankind to be redeemed from the power of sin. The Greek word for redeem is *exagorazo*. It means to recover from the power of another. Humankind had to be recovered from the power of sin.

The passage in Romans 3:23 shows the condition of humankind under the power of sin. It says, "All have sinned and come short of the glory of God." The Greek word for 'come short' is *hustereo*. It means to lack. Humankind lacks the glory God created within it in the beginning. The glory is not as complete as it once was. Genesis 1:26 states that God created man in His image and in His likeness. We learn from Scripture that God's image is one of glory (God is glorious). Scriptures found in Exodus 15:11, 1 Chronicles 29:13, Psalm 76:4, Isaiah 30:30, Luke 13:17, Philippians 3:21, Colossians 1:11, 1 Timothy 1:11, and Titus 2:13 all speak of the glorious attributes (qualities) of God. Isaiah 6:3, Ezekiel 10:4 and Habakkuk 3:3 all speak of God's glory having such a powerful radiance that it fills heaven and earth. We can see evidence of God's glory in John 1:14 (discussed earlier) as it records Christ becoming a man: "And the Word was made flesh, and dwelt among us, (and *we beheld his glory*, the glory as of the only begotten of the Father,) full of grace and truth." (Emphasis added.)

Dr. David Platt, pastor of The Church at Brook Hills in Birmingham, Alabama, once explained the condition of humankind excellently at a youth convention on Jekyll Island, Georgia. His message was titled the *Imago Dei* (Latin for 'Image of God'). He explained how the glory of God was imaged in man so that man was a mirror reflecting God's glory. We notice this in 2 Corinthians 3:18. It reads, "But we all, with unveiled face, beholding as in a mirror the glory of the Lord, are being transformed into the same image from glory to glory, just as from the Lord, the Spirit." That image of God was perfectly reflected in us until sin tarnished (as Dr. Platt states) that image so now God's glory did not reflect in humankind as it did in the beginning. After Adam's sin, humankind lacked the image (glory) of God, which it was created with. It's sort of like you trying to look into the mirror and fix your hair right after a hot shower. You can't see yourself well because of the steam. Steam has tarnished the mirror. God couldn't see Himself in humankind as well anymore because of the sin. Sin had tarnished God's mirror. The passage in Romans 3:23 just makes us aware of that.

The passage in Romans 6:23 lets us know the consequences for tarnishing the image God gave us. It gives the penalty for sin. It says, "For the wages of sin is death, but the gift of God is eternal life." The Greek word for wages as it is used here is *opsonion*, which means allowance or payment. The Greek word for death (as we mentioned in chapter 2) is *thanatos* and means separation. Notice on the Romans Road illustration how at the entrance to the Romans Road humankind was forced to depart from God (sent from the Garden of Eden) due to sin. That separation was the payment (wages) for sin. But God did not want it to stay that way, so He offered the gift of eternal life as the remainder of Romans 6:23 states.

The passage in Romans 5:8 states that even though humankind was condemned to be separated from God due to sin, God still loved humankind and made restitution (paid) for humankind to be reunited with Him. It says, "But God demonstrates His own love toward us, in that while we were yet sinners, Christ died for us." God did not stop loving humankind because of this separation that took place. It was punishment for a wrongdoing. But just like your parents don't stop loving you when they punish you by separating from you (such as sending you to your room), God did not stop loving humankind after separating Himself from them.

So, God offers us a way to get off of punishment. The passage in Romans 10:9 explains how to receive the gift of eternal life mentioned in Romans 6:23 and described in Romans 5:8. Romans 10:9 is the most important landmark on this Romans Road. This is how humankind can restore the relationship with God once enjoyed by the first two humans, Adam and Eve, before the separation caused by sin.

The process is very simple. The passage in Romans 10:9 says, "If you confess with your mouth Jesus as Lord, and believe in your heart that God raised Him from the dead, you will be saved." It is that simple. Just saying it and believing it. That restores the relationship between us and God. It means we can come out of our room of separation from God, because we are no longer grounded in sin. It removes the tarnish (takes away the veil) which sin placed on the image of God within us so the image of God shines through again. 2 Corinthians 3:16 states, "but whenever a person turns to the Lord, the veil is taken away."

There has been a lot of discussion on what happens after a person is saved (obtains salvation or restores this relationship with God). We even discussed it chapter 2. Many theologians and church folks have written on and discussed the matter, such as how do we know; how do we act; how do we stay, etc. There are a lot of points made as to what the correct answers to these questions are, but none of those questions or answers will change the simplicity of God's plan of salvation. A person still only needs to confess with their mouth that Jesus is Lord and believe in their heart that God raised Him from the dead in order to obtain salvation. At that point, they have arrived at the end of the Romans Road. They now have a restored relationship with God through Jesus Christ.

The Scripture in Romans 8:1 lets us know what the end of that road looks like; and it looks really nice. As you see on our Romans Road Illustration, the 'Son' is shining brightly. Romans 8:1 states, "Therefore there is now no condemnation [guilt] for those who are in Christ Jesus." (Brackets added for clarity.) That means we no longer have that tarnished appearance to God. We no longer have the condemnation of separation from God that came about at the first occurrence of sin (Genesis 3:23); which was passed along to all humankind (Romans 5:8);

which caused condemnation on humankind (Romans 3:23, 6:23); which was accounted for by Christ (Romans 5:8); which can be taken away by humankind's confession and belief in Jesus Christ (Romans 10:9-10). Now He can look at us and see Himself, again. That is the point we all want to reach on the Romans Road. That's where we as Christians want those we evangelize to wound up.

Group Hug

We as individuals can help others get to that point on the Romans Road, but as groups we may offer an even more effective means of evangelism than individuals. Hebrew 10:25 teaches that Christians should come together to encourage one another. It states, "Not forsaking the assembling of ourselves together, as the manner of some is; but exhorting [encouraging] one another: and so much the more, as ye see the day approaching." (Brackets added for clarity.)

Groups can evangelize in several different ways. Of course, there is group Bible Study, which can take place at a church, in a home, on a school campus, at a library, at a bookstore, in a park or almost anywhere. Groups are effective, for those who don't know Christ, because there are normally more experienced Christians around who can answer questions that arise during those discussions. There are more opportunities for giving correct answers and sharing encouraging testimonies. We just tend to feed off each other's energy and generate energy for others when evangelizing in a group setting.

The practice of grouping together to help one another has proven to be effective even outside of the Christian environment. Psychology professors and professionals train their students in the art of conducting 'group therapy'. The American Psychology Association even accredits (certifies; endorses) individuals and organizations to offer training in group therapy. That's just more proof grouping together to help one another works in improving an individual's condition.

Evangelism looks to improve an individual's Spiritual condition. You might state, then, that when it is done in groups it is a form of group therapy. In fact, group evangelism has been successful in the Christian environment much longer than group therapy has been recognized in the psychological setting. Again, Hebrews 10:25 gives us evidence of this. We Christians have been conducting group therapy as a means of evangelism since the Bible days. So you might say psychology can thank us for the idea. You're welcome, psychologists.

Kids will be Kids

Finally, another means of evangelism is through youth reaching other youth. There is a familiar saying among Christians that goes, "Sheep beget sheep." I don't know where it came from, but it makes good sense. It means that sheep are the ones who reproduce sheep; not goats, or cows or any other animal. I know we hear about scientists cloning sheep, but if they are, then everything they need to do so still comes from another sheep. Youth are best suited for reaching other youth–not young adults, not middle-aged adults, and not seniors. We grown folks like to think we are better at it, but we aren't.

To be a young evangelist is perhaps the most effective way to spread the gospel among other youth. Dean Finley states, "An informal survey of your church will reveal that 50 to 70 percent of them [church members] accepted Jesus as their Lord and Savior before reaching the age of twenty."[11] (Brackets added for clarity.) Such a statistic should make us think youth are very interested in evangelism. We know from experience youth prefer hanging out with and listening to other young folks versus hanging around and listening to us old folks.

There are several means by which you can evangelize other youth. Certainly, the church program should include space and time for you to participate in the service. This is very effective in gaining the interest of youth who may be visiting your church (or a church) for the first time. If they see you involved and interested in serving God, they are more apt to want to know God and serve Him.

If at all possible, youth should be allowed to have a separate worship service. If your church doesn't have a youth church service; you should talk to someone in church leadership about starting one. Youth in this environment are able to more freely exercise their gifts and grow their relationship with God. Of course, these youth services should have Christian adults supervising and assisting in them. As much as you may hate it, mature supervision still needs to be in place. There are still some things you haven't learned or don't understand, which require adult experience and know-how. Don't discount (ignore) the effectiveness experience of the *grey heads*.

Still, it's best for youth to have some ownership in the way they worship. Several authors have conducted research and determined that a mostly youth-centered learning environment is more effective in reaching youth than the traditional adult learning environment. Wesley Black, Chap Clark, and Melan Nel are three of them. They state in their book, *Four Views of Youth Ministry and the Church*, "This approach recognizes that there are cultural barriers that separate adolescents from adults. This is not only true of the secular world, but also the world of churched young people."[12]

Recreational activities are also effective means of evangelizing youth. All you need to do is invite some friends or acquaintances to your activities who don't know Christ as Lord. The activities can be in the form of hosting a sporting event or attending one as a group. They can also be outdoor adventures, such as scouting, hiking, fishing, or something along those lines. But, of course, not everybody likes those activities. So, they can also be sightseeing or movie-going or something a bit less adventurous. They can be movie nights, Superbowl Sunday, or a number of other events hosted at your church. They can also be lunch or dinner outings with a group of folks.

Remember the lunch discussion between Person1, Person2, and I in chapter two? That was an evangelizing moment. Even though, Person2 did not appear to show interest in learning more about Christ at the lunch outing, they were exposed to Him. Who knows what they pondered when they left there. I don't know what became of that conversation with Person2, but Person1 and I had several more conversations about what Christianity really is, what our relationship to God through Christ really should be, and how we portray that relationship to others. I came to learn that Person1 really did have an understanding of God. They stated they really had a relationship with Jesus Christ, and I believe it was a genuine statement. Of course, we don't have any right to judge whether or not a person is saved anyway, but we can tell if the person sounds sincere when making the claim. Person1 really sounded sincere. I was so relieved to hear Person1 confess that.

Person1 did not read the Bible much (that's a statement they made, not my conviction). For that reason, they could not piece together certain responses to situations based on Biblical principles. I believe this is why Person1 would not commit to being a Christian in front of Person2. Person1 really was trying not to offend or cause Person2 to stumble due to their comments. Perhaps Person1 did not realize there is as much danger in under-publicizing one's faith (being afraid to talk about it) as there is in over-publicizing it (offending people when you do talk about it).

Person1 and I would talk whenever they had a situation or question they wished to deal with or answer from a Biblical perspective. One day I gave an answer to one of Person1's question that must have been either obvious to them or intriguing (fascinating). As soon as I gave the answer, they said, "That's it! I'm going to the bookstore and pick out a study Bible. Come and help me find a good one." You can't imagine how good that statement made me feel! I wanted to pick up Person1 and carry them to that bookstore. Then I came to my senses. One: that would look pretty silly. Two: I probably wouldn't have made it (the store was a few blocks from our workplace. Besides, it wasn't even lunch time yet, so we couldn't go at that very moment anyway. So, I suggested to Person1 that we wait until lunch time; and I suggested to myself (silently) that we both walk. I had calmed down a bit by then.

I got an even bigger thrill a few weeks later, though, when Person1 called me into their office and said, "You got a minute? Sit down. Sit down." I didn't know whether to be excited or scared, but I sat down and tried not to look afraid.

Person1 explained they had been taking Scriptures that were often quoted in church or by churchgoers and trying to determine what these Scriptures really meant. Person1 wanted to really understand what all the clichés (popular phrases) were about. They started with the most familiar clichés first. They stated one, not verbatim (not word for word), then said it was often misquoted or misused. Actually, the phrase Person1 used is, "It was contextually incorrect."

I almost fell out of my chair. For one thing, I was so happy to see Person1's new found interest in the Word of God. They were taking a disciplined effort in getting to know God better and it showed. Not only were they holding meaningful conversation about Scripture, but they were also excited to do so.

I was also thrilled to see that God was confirming what His Word says and what this entire book emphasizes: If we work to get a good understanding of who God is, it will improve our relationship with God. We can then share that knowledge with others. This can correct others' misunderstandings of God or help them improve their relationship with God (or start one with Him if they don't already have one). All of this increases our faith and increases (or begins) their faith as well. If we share the knowledge of God, it will have a very positive impact on our lives and on the lives of others. In some cases we might be totally unaware of how much impact it is having such as with Person2. Other times it will be as clear as the impact seen in Person1.

When we host events in a Christian environment or in a Christian manner, we can enjoy them just as much as in a secular environment/manner. The only difference in ours' and those in a secular environment is we begin with recognition of and praise to God and you end the same. And we make sure nothing takes place in between that would dishonor God. In our recognition of God, we present the plan of salvation in some fashion (it doesn't have to be formal at all). Those friends or acquaintances we have invited who are not saved will have an opportunity to learn who Christ is and accept Him as Lord.

The fact that they have enjoyed the fellowship during the activities makes them less apprehensive of accepting Christ. The reason is they have learned Christianity doesn't have to be lifeless and liturgical (the formal steps we follow during church service). They see that we Christians are just as fun and loving (and sometimes crazy) as other folks.

Conclusion

Matthew 9:37-38 says, "Then He [Jesus] said to His disciples, 'The harvest is plentiful, but the workers are few. Therefore beseech the Lord of the harvest to send out workers into His harvest.'" (Brackets added for clarity.) No born-again believer will deny there is a need for evangelism in our world, in our country, and even in our churches. It is also evident that God has prepared and made available effective ways for achieving the goal of evangelism. Those means may be employed by individuals or groups and are especially effective among the younger generation.

Evangelism is the lifeblood of Christianity. If Christianity is to continue–and it most certainly shall continue until God's plan is completed–then evangelism must take precedence (come first). If the numbers of those who accept the Christian faith are to increase, then our evangelistic efforts must increase as well. Each Christian should have the mind of Christ, which is the will of God: Each of us should desire that no man, woman, boy or girl perishes, but rather are saved by God grace. Each of us should be eager to be an evangelist. This is the only way for us to get the knowledge of God (the truth of the Gospel) out to those who do not know it or do not believe it. You can see by the numbers and percentages presented that there are a lot of people who don't know or don't believe the Gospel.

Evangelism doesn't have to be hard. It does not have to be formal. It just has to be done with a purpose. That purpose is to share with somebody who God/Jesus really is. That's the whole gist (idea) of evangelism. Get the message of Jesus Christ to folks so they can make an intelligent decision on whether or not they want to know Him better. Prayerfully they will want to, but your part in evangelism is not to determine whether they will or not. That's their decision. If they accept Christ, you can't take the claim for them doing so. If they don't accept Christ, you shouldn't take the blame for their not doing so. If you have shared the knowledge of God to them according to what the Bible says, then you have been a good evangelist.

You don't have to worry if you are evangelizing like others have done it, either. Just do it–excuse me Nike–the rest will take care of itself. You don't even have to call it evangelism if you don't want to. It won't change your intent if you share the knowledge of God without calling it evangelism. You just need to make certain what you share is completely in agreement with what the Bible offers. Call it what you want, but make sure you share it in a way that folks know why you believe what you believe. Share it in a way that they will be inclined to believe. This introduces us to our next subject: Christianity as a belief system.

4 PROVING THE KNOWLEDGE OF GOD

"To be *dogmatic* in explaining something simply means to be *deliberate* in presenting it correctly." (Dr. Doris Rash-Konneh)

Upon This Rock

This chapter discusses Christianity as a belief system. Your belief system is your worldview. It is how you view or understand the world around you based on all you believe to be true. It's how you put reasoning to all the chaos that goes on. It's how you answer questions like "Is abortion wrong?" or "Should I support this cause or that cause?" or even "What's wrong with drinking, cursing, smoking a little marijuana?"

According to Norman Geisler and Peter Bocchino, the authors of *Unshakable Foundations*, a worldview is "a set of beliefs, a model that attempts to explain all of reality, not just some aspect of it."[1] So a worldview doesn't just answer, "Where do babies come from" or "Why is the sky blue?" It's doesn't just deal with how you feel about politics or war. It really answers the hard question, "What is the meaning of life?" So as you develop your worldview, your answer to the meaning of life, you need to be careful who you accept input from for your answer. Yeah, you will have to ask some questions before you can develop your own answer, but you need ask or at least listen to the right people when forming your answer. That's what Solomon, tells us in Proverbs 23:1-7. I'm using the KJV here.

[1]When thou sittest to eat with a ruler, consider diligently what is before thee: [2]And put a knife to thy throat, if thou be a man given to appetite. [3]Be not desirous of his dainties: for they are deceitful meat. [4]Labour not to be rich: cease from thine own wisdom. [5]Wilt

thou set thine eyes upon that which is not? for riches certainly make themselves wings; they fly away as an eagle toward heaven. ⁶Eat thou not the bread of him that hath an evil eye, neither desire thou his dainty meats: ⁷For as he thinketh in his heart, so is he: Eat and drink, saith he to thee; but his heart is not with thee.

You may want to read the NASB with this, but I wanted to present the seriousness of the matter as captured in the KJV. There is a grave warning presented here by Solomon. He warns us in verse six to, "Eat not the bread of him that hath an evil eye." To eat the bread of or break bread with someone back in the Bible days meant more than just to share a meal. Breaking bread or mealtime to those folks was the ultimate symbol of socializing. It was fellowshipping and learning of each other's ways. It was how a group showed a person or group they were accepted into their circle. It was how a person or group showed they wanted to be accepted.

Those people whom Solomon refers to as "...hath an evil eye" are just people who see nothing wrong with doing wrong. Those are folks who look at ungodliness as no big deal. It doesn't bother them a bit to do bad stuff. They have an 'if it feels good do it' mentality. It doesn't take long for you to recognize when people have this attitude toward life. Their worldview is certainly not the Christian worldview. They see things in a different light (or they have an evil eye view as Solomon says). You can listen to them talk for a while or pay attention to the things they like to do and notice an evil eye view on life.

With this in mind, we can understand why in verse one of Proverbs 23, Solomon warns us to pay close attention to what is being presented when we break bread or associate with others. Listen carefully before we decide if what is being discussed is worth adding to our worldview. In other words, be sure what you are involving yourself in does not contradict your belief system.

Verse two sounds scary, but all it's saying is if you're the gullible (easy to fool) type, then don't join in the conversation. Don't mingle with that crowd. Don't submit yourself to the ideas and actions being presented by them. Just walk away or better yet avoid those folks. As old folks say, "Nip it in the bud."

In verse seven, Solomon says as a person thinks in their hearts, so are they. If we think it's okay to do bad things, then we will do bad things, which makes us a bad person. It's that simple. If we continuously hang around ungodliness, sooner or later we will think in our hearts, these people are not as bad as folks say they are. It's called becoming desensitized to the ungodliness. Remember, "...as he thinketh in his heart..." If we allow ourselves to become desensitized to ungodliness, we will believe in our hearts there's nothing wrong with doing wrong. Then we will become ungodly because we have determined within our hearts that ungodliness really isn't so bad. Don't get comfortable with strange philosophies and ungodly advice. Psalm 1:1 warns us of this. It states, "How blessed is the man who does not walk in the counsel of the wicked..." Bad counsel can easily get taken in as part of your worldview and affect how you view things and how you respond to things–how you act and how you react. It could change your Christian worldview into something else.

A Solid Structure

Christianity is a very solid worldview, one with a foundation that does not erode in the battering rains or the gusty winds of skepticism (doubt). If you were to closely evaluate some worldviews, you'll see they make claims even their originators (those who came up with the view) have doubts about. Some other worldviews leave their followers with a sense of hopelessness or uncertainty about the meaning of life. It is because these worldviews are founded on theories or beliefs (basic elements) that are not very sound.

That's not the case with Christianity. Our Christian worldview is like a rock. When Jesus said that he was building his church on a rock and even the gates of hell wouldn't be able to triumph over it (see Matthew 16:18), that's what He meant. Christianity started strong and stays strong. Nothing proves truer than Christianity. That means we can look at other worldviews and see where they fall short of the truth, but when we compare Christianity in the same light, it holds its ground. I don't say that with arrogance or attitude. I'm just simply stating the facts.

This chapter exposes some non-truths in humankind's knowledge (the ideas that support other worldviews) which attempt to move Christians away from God's knowledge (the facts that should support our worldview). It shows where in some cases humankind attempts to replace knowledge of God with its own. This happens in three areas where we often attempt to answer the question, "What's the meaning of life?" These areas are critical components of one's worldview. The critical components are moral values, the origin of life, and how we deal with societal issues. In many cases, at least concerning these three components, what much of secular academia teaches contradicts greatly with (goes against) Biblical truth.

The object of this chapter is to represent why each critical component either holds up or washes away under scrutiny (analysis or close examination). As a form of analysis, Christianity will be compared to some other worldviews that strongly contradict the Christian worldview. You will see how other worldviews' critical components not only contradict the Bible, but themselves as well. This should help you really see what they have to offer.

I will make every effort to stay objective (neutral). I know Christians often get the label of not being objective when it comes to discussing non-Christian topics. I am a Christian, so some of the things stated may seem somewhat dogmatic in nature. That means there are some cases where there is no place for middle ground, so there is no reason for arguments or doubts, so I won't offer any. Some things are just Biblical truth, so it will not agree with non-truth no matter how much we debate it. This is due to the Law of non-contradiction we discussed earlier.

Just the Facts

I make this statement not to justify a bend toward subjectivity (I'm not making a case for being biased toward Christianity–even though personally I am biased). My bias will be held in check so as to create a basis for not deviating from the truth. The term dogmatic has been bestowed an unwarranted negative connotation–it has been given a bad rap–especially as it applies to Christians expressing ourselves. Back in the first chapter, Person1 and Person2 expressed what many non-Christians express: 'Christians don't want to hear anyone's truth, but their own'.

This is labeled as dogmatism and gives an appearance of self-righteousness, but that's not the case. In essence, dogmatism is essential if one is to start with the facts and remain in them as one builds a case for truth. That goes for anybody, Christian or not. Again, that's all part of the first law of principles. The first law of principles applies to Biblical knowledge just as much as it does to science, math, philosophy or any other form of knowledge-gathering. This law requires a certain level of dogmatism–staying with the facts.

Dr. Doris Rash-Konneh, a professional editor and adjunct professor at Atlanta, Georgia's Interdenominational Theological Center, once made the statement, "To be dogmatic in explaining something means simply to be deliberate in presenting it accurately." She is saying if you intend to stick with the truth, then you can't be vacillating (changing, switching, wishy washy) in your statement of facts, regardless of your personal feelings or prior misunderstandings. If you do, somewhere along the way you're going to slip away from the truth.

The validity (truth) of Dr. Rash-Konneh's statement is reinforced when paralleled with Dr. David L. Mape's (another professor at Luther Rice University) teachings on the "straight line" approach to presenting truth accurately. He advocated (encouraged) presenting the Word of God as pure science (proven truth instead of just some theory). He expressed that anyone who presents the truth should use the straight-line approach, which as he says, "does not assume but proves the truth."

'Pure' science takes this approach and does not deviate (swerve or change somehow) based on some person's or a group of people's theories, beliefs, or personal convictions. I agree with Dr. Rash-Konneh, Dr. Mapes and the scientific process. All knowledge-gathering, knowledge-exploration, and knowledge-sharing should take the straight-line approach. One should be dogmatic in presenting knowledge. So, in this discussion of the three critical components of a worldview (moral values, the origin of life, and dealing with societal issues), this book will stick to those principles. If I appear to be biased or dogmatic, it is because I intend to stick with the truth.

Mulling Over Morality: What Does Morality Mean?

The first critical element of worldviews we will discuss is morality. How do our views on morality affect our overall worldview? A brief discussion on the subject should reveal this.

Merriam-Webster defines morality as "the conformity to ideals of right."[2] In simpler terms, it is acting in accordance with how you think you should conduct yourself. It is your character. This is an important element of your worldview, because this is the governing agent (driving force) by which you feel you should conduct yourself as an individual, as a community, as a country, as a race, or with whatever body of members you associate yourself.

In Regards to Relativism

The first worldview we'll examine to discover if it has an amiable (acceptable) moral character at its foundation is Relativism. Relativism is the view that truth is relative and not absolute. Relative means the answer may vary depending on where you are and who you ask. So, according to the relativistic view, in different places and times, two contradicting statements may be equally true. The same goes for moral values. Two contradicting moral values can be equally good, according to this view.

We're going to use observations from an article by Derek L. Phillips published in the *Cognitive Relativism & Social Science Journal*[3] in this section so we can obtain well-prepared data for this discussion. Phillip's article on Lawrence Kohlberg's theory of moral development will be the focal point (center of attention). Kohlberg and a few other really smart folks conducted twenty years of longitudinal study on moral development. Longitudinal study means they have researched groups of subjects over a long period of time. So, Kohlberg is regarded as a subject matter expert in this area of study. This might get a little boring, so grab another Mountain Dew® or something and stay focused.

Phillips begins his article confirming the growth in popularity of "relativistic styles of thought (227)" in the area of morality. He lets the readers know that although relativism is becoming more popular among the general population, the experts still don't think much of it. Phillips makes the statement, "Despite the considerable influence of relativistic styles of thought, the dominant position in moral philosophy today rejects relativism altogether (227)." The biggest case against Relativism's moral system, then, is the experts in this field say this style of thinking is not beneficial.

I can almost hear you saying, "Oooh! Aaah!" Okay, so this doesn't fascinate you. It doesn't do much for me either, but hang in there with me. We have to provide researched information here, because we want our point to go over as factual and not as just our opinion. We don't want to appear to be stuck in our own philosophical world. We want representation from all parties. This allows anyone who opposes our understanding of the facts to really have a means of analyzing it before making a decision on what to believe. So I'm going to use a few more academic terms. I'm going to draw this thing out a little, but go through it with me. Believe me; it's just as boring to me as it is to you.

Phillips continues his discussion on relativism by offering viewpoints of Theorists such as Rawls (1971), Nozick (1974), Dworkin (1979), and Gewirth (1978). These are guys (and gals) who all subscribe to (believe in) the Kantian approach to morality. It appears they believe "all human beings have equal moral value, this value lying in their capacity for reflections, for exercising judgments, and for utilizing their capacity for choice (227)." They seem to think a person's ability to rationalize is the underlying code for their moral conduct. A little plainer: they say we can think things through enough to know and do the right thing–without being trained, taught or told. We have the ability within ourselves to make good decisions. That's their stance.

Each of the theorists (philosophers) mentioned above offers mechanisms for staying in line with their theory or as Phillips puts it, "eliminating the influence of special interests, values, and so forth (228)." They give parameters which others must stay within if others are to see things their way. In other words, they say if this case is true and if that case is true, then our statements are true. To help you understand this better (not that you don't already) let me say it like this: That's sort of like someone making the statement, "It's *definitely* going to rain today!" Then they add: *if* enough clouds gather together; and *if* they are the right type of clouds; and *if* they gather more moisture than they can hold; and *if* the wind doesn't blow them away before the moisture releases. Well yeah, it will rain *if* all these conditions are true. You don't have to be a meteorologist to make that statement with boldness.

The philosophers provide themselves a safety net (my observation, not Phillips') for those subjects who fall off the theoretical tightrope they have erected for them. (They have made themselves a loophole for any cases that just may prove their theory false.) To create such a pungent caveat proves agnostic. (This shows they seriously doubt themselves.) The theorists are not committing to their own theory if they have to create scenarios which make their statement true or if they ignore or block out factors known to exist. Like I stated before, this is one of the accusations I've often heard made against Christians. Some feel we leave out information or create situations to make ourselves appear to be right. I don't mean to sound judgmental, but that's very hypocritical of them.

Phillips appears to agree with the fact that these theorists are not being true to themselves. He makes the statement, "Of course, they have quite different notions of what constitutes the appropriate point of view (228)." Their unwillingness to commit to their theory creates an environment ripe for cultivating (growing; developing) relativism even though they claim total rejection to relativism. If a theory has to be situational to be credible, then it follows along the lines of relativity. In other words, its truth is in the eyes of the beholder. Are they saying what one person sees as truth may not be truth for another, yet they both can be correct? I think that's what they're saying. I have to mention the First Law of Principles, again. Two opposites cannot be equal.

Phillips offers a lot of boring information on Kohlberg's moral theory. He continues that there are "five (or six, depending on the status of his scoring manual (230))" stages to Kohlberg's moral development theory. Phillips addresses the first three in the article referenced here. His purpose, I assume, is to discuss enough of them to demonstrate the pattern Kohlberg's theory takes on. Each stage takes shape in accordance with the person's situational conflict (the problem they face at that moment). Again, that seems strikingly familiar to relativism, but Kohlberg denies being a Relativist.

Kohlberg argues that a person will *fail to make* morally good decisions based on their *moral immaturity* and *make* morally good decisions, based on their *moral maturity*. He claims the maturation process (the way you get better at making morally good decisions) is to progressively replace immoral values with moral values. A term we can build for making immoral decisions [based on words used in the article] is epistemologically *inferior* logical operation. We can call making moral decisions the epistemologically *superior* logical operation.

Don't get caught up in trying to fully understand or be able to recite these reusable labels. I just want to give you something to associate the entire message with. Remember, preachers and teachers love to offer reusable labels for their messages. Keep them in the back of your memory bank or highlight them here. When you get to a point where you have an opportunity to discuss this, you can whip out these big words and sound extremely intelligent–not that you don't already sound extremely intelligent. People tend to listen to you more closely when you use witty words. We'll call it a trick of the academic trade.

I know there's a whole lot of mumbo jumbo going on here, but the issue with this whole relativism theory should be fairly clear. Each stage is based on the condition or position of the person's own internal moral belief system (what their own reasoning makes them believe is okay). How can a person mature enough to produce superior epistemological logic (know how to replace bad moral values with good moral values), when they do not go outside of their immature moral system to find those more mature moral values. Their system is currently too immature to make good decisions, yet it will still decide what's best when the time comes?

If there are no 'nutrients coming in' (no feeding of what is moral), then there is no way for the immature moral system to grow to maturity. It's the same as with your physical body. If you don't provide it with nourishment, it will never mature. If you don't provide your mind with knowledge, it will never grow. If you don't feed your moral system with good moral values, your moral system will never mature.

Relativism and Kohlberg's moral theory, an apparent derivative (obvious form) of Relativism, both have foundational issues in their element of moral character. They did not include a logical operation by which the person's internal moral character might improve itself. There is no way for the moral system to improve itself without some outside influence. This theory does not qualify as a good base element in one's worldview.

How Feminism Finds It

The next worldview we'll examine to see if it has a good moral foundation for building a worldview is Feminism. We're won't be examining feminism from a male/female (or female/male) struggle for dominance standpoint. We are only concerned with the relativism aspect of feminism. We'll look at its basic understanding of moral character. Phillips' article will be used in this section as well. I know what you're thinking, "Not that guy again!" Hey, Phillips has some good information. We just have to take our time and decipher (make sense of) the academic expressions–you know, big words.

Phillips includes Feminist and theorist, Carol Gilligan's point of view, because it opposes the view held by Kohlberg (the guy we just talked about). Gilligan is a former student of Kohlberg as Phillips points out. As I hope you'll see, this irony further weakens the foundation of moral character in relativism as well as Kohlberg's moral theory. Kohlberg's own student disagrees with his theory.

The premise for Gilligan's variance (the basis for her disagreement) with Kohlberg is she feels males' moral decisions are justice-oriented, but females' moral decisions are care-oriented. In other words, she feels males naturally judge things based on the different situations, so their moral character is based on their desire to compare things. Females, on the other hand, are natural caregivers so their moral character is based on their desire to care for everyone.

Phillips gives Gilligan's account on page 233: "While males worry about people interfering with each other's rights, females worry about the possibility of omission, of not helping others when you could help them (Gilligan 1982)." Gilligan's assault on Kohlberg's theory washes away at Kohlberg's foundation. Phillips expresses this weakening effect:

Many feminist philosophers have seen Gilligan's work as also raising fundamental questions about moral philosophy. If girls and women do not generally follow the principled morality advocated by Kohlberg and by moral philosophers in the Kantian tradition, then the adequacy of the general Kantian conception of morality is obviously called into question (233).

Okay, you probably either skipped over the quotes up there or all you saw was, "Blah, blah, blah, blah, blah." It took me a few times before I could stay focused long enough to get it, too. Every now and then I would wake up and realize I was supposed to be reading something and had to start over.

Since you probably don't want to read through it again, I will try to restate it clearer (just in case you glazed over it). Phillips is saying that this disagreement between Gilligan and Kohlberg has caused some feminists to adopt a "completely relativistic stance concerning Gilligan's findings and their implications for moral psychology and moral philosophy (234)."

Here is where this whole relative moralist thing implodes (here is where it defeats itself): In an attempt to redact (take away) male-imposed errors in Kohlberg's moral theory, Gilligan has reverted to acute (strong) relativism, the thing her teacher and mentor, Kohlberg, opposed from the start. In simpler terms, Gilligan's attempt to improve or correct Kohlberg's theory destroyed both her theory and his.

Okay, let me try and clean all this up a little bit before we move on. Here's the Soap Opera version: Kohlberg wanted to prove his theory was not a form of relativism, because relativism does not have good moral character at its core. In doing so, he left out consideration for the differences in how men and women rationalize when making moral decisions (according to Gilligan, one of his students). So, Gilligan made corrections to Kohlberg's theory based on her Feministic beliefs. Her corrections proved Kohlberg's theory really is Relativistic in nature, placing Kohlberg in conflict with his own theory. Remember he says he does not agree with Relativism. Her theory is rooted in his, so she really disagrees with her own theory, too.

Those Relativistic Theorists have contradicted themselves and because of that, their theory has imploded. I believe Gilligan is stranded on a theoretical island; Gilligan, Kohlberg, Skipper and anybody else who tries to keep this moralistic theory afloat. (I'm just fishing for a joke at their expense.) It is evident that neither relativistic moral theory nor the feminist version of it qualifies as a good base element for moral character in one's worldview.

How Christians Critique It

Now, let's take a look at Christianity's foundational element for moral character. Probably by now, both advocate readers (those who agree with me) and adversarial readers (those who disagree with me) have been awaiting this section to see if I will maintain an unbiased and objective approach while critiquing my own preferred worldview. The intended objectivity will be maintained; however, bias against the Christian worldview must be addressed, again, to ensure the reader does the same.

It is common to see those who profess (claim) to hold to the Christian worldview engaging in practices which do not align with Christian principles (morals in this case). In other words, there are many people who talk Christianity but don't live it out. Those folks who mishandle Christian principles do not provide non-Christians with a good representation of Christianity. In such cases, other worldview holders (non-Christians) obtain a distorted view of Christian principles or moral standards. They've been given the wrong impression. The observer sees the professed Christian's partial commitment to the Christian worldview and assumes it to be how the entire Christian community conducts itself. They think that's how all Christians act. Not so. Those folks who claim to be Christians but do all sorts of immoral stuff don't represent all Christians.

For the record, the Bible teaches against this noncommittal approach to maintaining Christian moral values. It says we shouldn't give bad representation of Christianity. It states we should be, "giving no cause for offense in anything, so that the ministry [sharing of the Christian worldview] will not be discredited (2 Corinthians 6:3– brackets added for clarity)." Dr. David P. Gushee makes observation of this type of behavior in some Christians in an article published by the *Christianity Today* Magazine. He states: "We [Christians] are indeed morally sloppy, and I think it is because we have embraced truncated [partial] versions of the Christian faith that have trained us to be this way."[4] (Brackets added for clarity.) He's saying we take on some of the moral responsibilities of being a Christian, but not all of them. Some Christians don't hold true to all the Christian values, so they should not be used as examples of what true Christian values really are.

So as to not promote bias, then, true Christian principles will be employed in this discussion, rather than the 'truncated versions' displayed by many professing Christians today. We will be examining Christianity at the core, not based on what you might see in the activities of some professing Christians. The same method was applied in the previous discussions. How Kohlberg, Gilligan and others lived out their principles was not discussed, but rather the basic properties of their theories.

A review of an article published in the *Journal of Economic Issues* by Dr. Charles Clark, Professor of Business at St. John's University in New York, shows us how to examine Christianity at the core when comparing it to theories. In fact, Dr. Clark refers to Christianity, in this case, as "a theoretical system in its purest and most elementary form."[5] The article, "Christian Morals and the Competitive System Revisited," analyzes Thorstein Veblen's essay, "Christian Morals and the Competitive System."

Don't worry; I'm not going to flood you with a whole lot of academic jargon (terms), again. Dr. Clark gives a great deal of explanation in this article. The bottom line, though, is that at the core of Christianity is a foundation for building moral character which cannot be shaken. To avoid casting a shadow of bias on his debate for Christianity (to keep the critics honest), he reveals the same principle is held to some extent in other faiths (such as, Islam, Buddhism, Judaism, Confucianism, and Hinduism). Although those faiths have some principles which do not align with Christianity, Dr. Clark includes them in his article just to prove he is taking an unbiased approach at explaining core Christian values.

There is a great deal of theological discussion in Dr. Clark's article. In it, theologians take several different approaches at determining the moral character at the foundation of Christianity. Again, I'm not going to talk through all that. We can resolve the whole matter quickly and simply. All we have to do is approach the discussion directly from what the Bible says constitutes core Christian moral character. The moral character at the foundation of Christianity is love–the love of God and the love of other people.

Jesus Christ (the founder of Christianity–but of course you know that) is recorded by three different writers in the Bible as saying that every command ever given by God can be wrapped up into two mandates (two directives or commands): 'Love God as much as you possibly can and love each other as much as you love yourselves' (paraphrasing–see Matthew 22:39, Mark 12:31, and Luke 10:27).

Therefore, the best way to describe the critical element of moral character at the core of Christianity is to say that love is its basis.

Christianity differs greatly from the theories we just discussed in matters concerning what regulates our moral character. The others rely on an individual's epistemological (natural) ability to discern (distinguish) between moral and immoral character. That is to say, they have their own moral compass. They have their own way of determining what is right or wrong. Christianity requires all individuals to use God's moral compass–love.

The influence of love transcends (goes beyond) the personal levels of epistemologically logical operations that Kohlberg's theory lacks. The influence of love also transcends any gender-related principles which Gilligan suggests would affect those epistemologically logical operations. Therefore, worldviews with foundations of relativism and feministic relativism wash away under objective criticism and so does the moral character they are built upon, while Christianity's foundational moral character of love stands firm.

Opinions on Origin: What Darwinism Deems

The next critical element of a worldview up for discussion is origin of life. How do our views on how life began affect our overall worldview? Again, a brief discussion on the subject should reveal this.

Darwinism (a theory known as evolution) suggests that all of life originated from inanimate (non-living) matter. If you have attended public school in America and don't already know this, then you must have hibernated through every semester of science you've ever had. Well, it's time to wake up, because we're going to talk about old Darwin a little bit.

Gerald Skool gives a thorough outline of the theories and concepts taught in Darwinism in a book review published in the *Journal of College Science Teaching* titled, "The Nature of Science and the Study of Biological Evolution." What a cool name for a guy who writes articles in a journal for teachers, huh? According to Skool, "the experience of [a] five-year voyage on the [ship] Beagle influenced his [Darwin's] thinking. The concept of natural selection emerged from his experiences [and] observations"[6] (Brackets added for grammatical structure and clarity). The concept of natural selection proposes that species or groups of species adjust to their environment through the perpetuation of genetic changes best suited to their particular environment. In other words, plants and animals evolve to be better equipped to survive in whatever environment they are in. Natural selection is one of the core principles of the theory of evolution. Through the years, evolution was never proven. In fact, it has been disproven over the years.

Geisler and Bocchino have a very simple explanation of why Darwin was wrong about his theory on evolution. In their explanation, they quote Darwin in showing lack of confidence in his own theory. Darwin writes, "If it could be demonstrated that any complex organ existed, which could not possibly have been formed by numerous, successive, slight modifications [evolution], my theory would absolutely break down."[7] (Brackets added.) Now, this is Darwin talking. As a good scientist, he is making room for all information to be gathered and evaluated before determining his theory to be fact.

Geisler and Bocchino illustrate that science has discovered this complex organ. In doing so, they prove Darwin did not understand the complex nature of the cell. This is not a personal attack on Darwin. Darwin was a brilliant man. It just simply means the technology to expose the inner structure of the cell was not at Darwin's disposal when he was forming his theory. Geisler and Bocchino write:

It was not too long ago that the cell was considered to be a black box, a term used to describe an apparatus whose inner components are mysterious in that they are not observable or are incomprehensible... in the mid-1800s, the time of Charles Darwin, the cell was still a black box to Darwin and every other scientist... The question of how life works was not one that Darwin or his contemporaries [colleagues] could answer.[8] (Brackets added for clarity.)

The authors go on to describe the very complex build and operation of the cell. The cell is amazingly complex. There are eighteen distinctive components to the cell, if I am not mistaken and most of them I can't spell. There is a flurry of activity going on between those components. Darwin did not know all of this was going on inside of a single cell. He thought what he saw of the cell (the outer structure) was the tiniest element to life there was. It is not.

The authors explain the immense degree of information coded within each cell. They also show how scientists have proven with the technology they now have that the basic elements (particularly protein) found in the cell could not have survived the early stages of the earth's atmosphere. In one of his course lectures, Dr. Mapes explains the problem of achieving the first cell through the evolutionary theory. He shows how the makeup of the earth's early atmosphere at some stages, according to scientists, would have destroyed any protein present. He summed up his lecture on the matter saying, "In order for the first cell's protein synthesis process to work, there would have had to have been protein available in the earth's early atmosphere."[9] There was no protein to start the first cell.

Geisler and Bocchino also explain that paleontological evidence (fossil study) has not produced any evidence of staged life forms required for evolution. This was another area where Darwin doubted his own theory. Darwin wrote a chapter (Chapter 6) in his famed *The Origin of Species* entitled "Difficulties on Theory." After paleontology did not produce the evidence he had predicted, he wrote, "*Why*, if species have descended from other species by insensibly fine graduations [evolution], *do we not* everywhere *see innumerable transitional forms* [fossils of such]?"[10] (Brackets added for clarity. Emphasis added.) Again, Darwin stays true to the scientific process. He records both the positive and negative data surrounding his theory, so an informed analysis can be made on its validity. Concerning the new information found in cell formation and the missing information from paleontology, Geisler and Bocchino write: "All of the evidence shows that there are no objective scientific reasons why we ought to accept any form of the macroevolutionary model [evolution]."[11] (Brackets added.)

Nancy Pearcy, author of *Total Truth*, uses knowledge of key points in the Darwinist worldview to show how it implodes when true science is applied to it. She shows how various evolutionary arguments are purported (alleged) without scientific evidence and in some cases involve fraud (scams). Some of these are purported by Darwinists (followers of Darwin), but they don't appear to have been approved by Darwin, himself.

Pearcy provides drawings from public school textbooks depicting embryos from various animals alongside one of a human. Just in case you forgot, an embryo is an unborn, not-fully-formed human or animal–you know, still in the tummy. Each of the drawings looks very similar in their first stages of life–almost identical. She then offers some drawings that better represent the actual embryos at those same stages, and there are substantial differences in each embryo. So many, in fact, that there is no likeness in most cases. This misrepresentation in the textbooks gives an unfair advantage to Darwinism in its quest to be a foundation for understanding the origin of life.

Continuous use of fictitious drawings further exposes the fact that evolutionists tend to subdue the truth to promote their cause. Darwin's own admission to not having the complete truth, scientific discoveries since his theory was formulated, and deviation from science in representation of his theory prove this theory to be a flawed foundation for knowing the origin of life. Therefore, it does not qualify as a good base element in one's worldview.

What's Biblically Believable

Creationism suggests that non-life cannot produce life; therefore, the first group of life forms on earth had to be the creative result of a Super-intelligent Being. Creationism is the belief that the world and various forms of life were created by God out of nothing, in the way described in Genesis. Its scientific proof is the same science that disproves Darwin's evolution. The lowest form of life, the cell, proves too complex to have happened from the gradual, haphazard (random) gathering of molecules—as evolution suggests.

Since nature could not have performed the building of the first cell, something outside of nature (i.e., something Supernatural) must have. Science makes it obvious that there had to have been an 'Intelligent Designer'—as Pearcy terms it. Science also proves matter has not always existed but that it (the universe) had a definite beginning.

Geisler and Bocchino offer scientific evidence of this definite beginning. Their key arguing point in this is science's Second Law of Thermodynamics. Put in very non-scholastic terms, the Second Law of

Thermodynamics suggests that everything in nature has a beginning and an end. It doesn't address how the universe began, but it states that it began somehow and now moves toward its end through the process of increasing entropy.

Entropy is the measure of the disorder of a system. It is the understanding that all systems in nature eventually break down. The authors use a quote from Sir Arthur Eddington, a contemporary (he came along at the same time) of Albert Einstein and one-time professor at the University of Cambridge. Sir Eddington writes, "...if your theory is found to be against the Second Law of Thermodynamics, I can give you no hope; there is nothing for it but to collapse in deepest humiliation."[12] The universe itself is bound by this law (according to scientists), so then there had to have been a beginning, thus a Beginner. If there was a beginning, there must be an end as the Second Law of Thermodynamics suggests. Jesus states that heaven and earth will pass away (see Matthew 24:35, Mark 13:31, and Luke 21:33). Science's Second Law of Thermodynamics agrees with the Bible as it should.

The Bible states that in the beginning God created the heavens and the earth. Therefore, we as Christians believe Creationism to be the cause of the origin of life. There is absolutely no evidence in science which can contradict this truth, but there is evidence to support it–not that the Bible needs science's support. Since science proves Darwinism to be false and cannot disprove Creationism as truth, but rather supports it, then Christianity stands as the best foundation for building a worldview of the origin of life.

Sorting Societal Issues: Relativism Revisited

The final critical element of a worldview to discuss is views on how we deal with social issues. How do our views on dealing with societal issues affect our overall worldview? Once more, a brief discussion on the subject should reveal this.

In an earlier section in this chapter titled "Mulling Over Morality," we said subscription to (belief in) Relativism requires us to hold a view that ethical truths depend on the individuals and groups holding them. That means each individual's or group's perception of reality is based on his or her current environment (in this case, society). Put more plainly, a person or group makes the best decisions based on what that person or group believes is moral–supposedly.

If relativism is the foundation for handling societal issues, then that society will handle its issues with the perceived ethical conviction it has always held. It employs a vicious cycle of inner epistemologically logical operation (explained earlier). If every other society in the world sees the handling of an issue in a certain society as immoral, it will not matter to this society. The questionable society will still handle the issue as it has and continue to view its process for doing so as moral. For example, the rest of the world can think an act is inhumane (cruel), but if this society (be it a small group, organization, town, village, state, or country) thinks it is okay, then according to relativism, it is okay.

Geisler and Bocchino bring this point out in their discussion of the events that took place in Nazi Germany from 1933 to 1945. The society's epistemologically logical operation (ethical conviction) conveyed there was one superior race and that this race should prevail based on the idea of survival of the fittest. Apparently, they determined they were the ones who qualified as the fittest. Once they determined that, they decided to help nature along in its 'survival of the fittest' process by eliminating those who did not belong to their race.

Adolf Hitler, the ruler at the time, was a firm believer in Darwin's theories on evolution and natural selection. Geisler and Bocchino expose a little known fact that Darwin was a beholder of the idea of a superior race prior to Hitler. The authors offer a quote from both Theorists to show the similarity in their thinking:

Darwin–"By means of natural selection or the preservation of favoured [sic] races in the struggle for life."[13]

Hitler–"The superior race must not mate with the inferior races."[14]

I'm not implying that Darwin would have agreed with Hitler's idea of exterminating another race due to its perceived inferiority (a belief that another race is not as good as your own). Darwin felt nature would remove all inferior races. It simply illustrates that dealing with societal issues based on individuals' or groups' internally developed relative morals does not always prove to be good when compared to morals developed external to that society. There is no external check valve for what is moral or immoral in this circular, inner reasoning process within a society. Therefore, relativism is not a good base element for developing answers to societal issues.

Scriptures Scrutinized

In keeping with my pledge to remain objective, since the implication of genocide (massive killing) was offered in the Nazi Germany era discussion above, we will also address genocide in the Christian Bible. The Bible states that God instructed certain leaders to destroy entire countries or groups when they warred against them. God instructed those leaders to do so at a certain time in history for a certain reason: for judgment of those cultures' continuous, intentional infringement of the moral law of God (love) and because those societies were a threat to other societies. Nazism's genocidal intent to remove a race of people because of their perceived inferiority (a moral belief held internally by their societal environment) does not compare. To try and compare the two would not only try to reduce God's way of thinking to that of humankind's but also ignore the intentions of both.

Also, God's genocidal judgment took place before the existence of Christianity. According to the Bible, the law under which this judgment was carried out was fulfilled [resolved; dealt with successfully] by Christ. So, Christians should in no way be considered connected to genocidal movements. God has not given any of us the directive or the freedom to commit such acts against humankind. Any form of 'crusades' which follow such tendencies, calling themselves *Christian* Crusades, inappropriately label themselves as such.

As stated earlier, Christians' obligation under the moral law of God is to love others as much as they do themselves. The Bible makes this clear: "For the whole Law is fulfilled in one word [the original Greek term used was logo meaning (in this context): decree, mandate or order–so 'one mandate'], in the statement, 'YOU SHALL LOVE YOUR NEIGHBOR AS YOURSELF' (Galatians 5:14)." (Brackets added.) Under God's new Law (the mandate to love), Christianity does not encourage or consent to (agree with) genocide.

We can understand God no longer uses such genocidal measures if we understand the idea of the different dispensations outlined in the Bible and the different covenants (agreements) between God and humankind during each of those dispensations of time. God may have begun dealing with humankind in one way concerning our moral conduct, but as he matured the relationship He has with us, his way of dealing with us (and the covenants [agreements] associated with those dealings) changed somewhat.

God did not change His mind on how He felt about our moral attitude toward Him in all this. He simply presented different avenues of relating to us and responding to our moral character in each covenant. So then, covenants were not done away with; they were just nestled into a new covenant or agreement. Consequently, the past covenants' requirements were absorbed into (fulfilled by) the most current covenant. Without defining and discussing each covenant in detail (that would take a long time and you would be bored with it all), I'll just offer a visual representation of the nesting of these covenants.

The graphic layout is mine, but the explanation of nested covenants came from one of my professors' lectures. I can't remember which one.

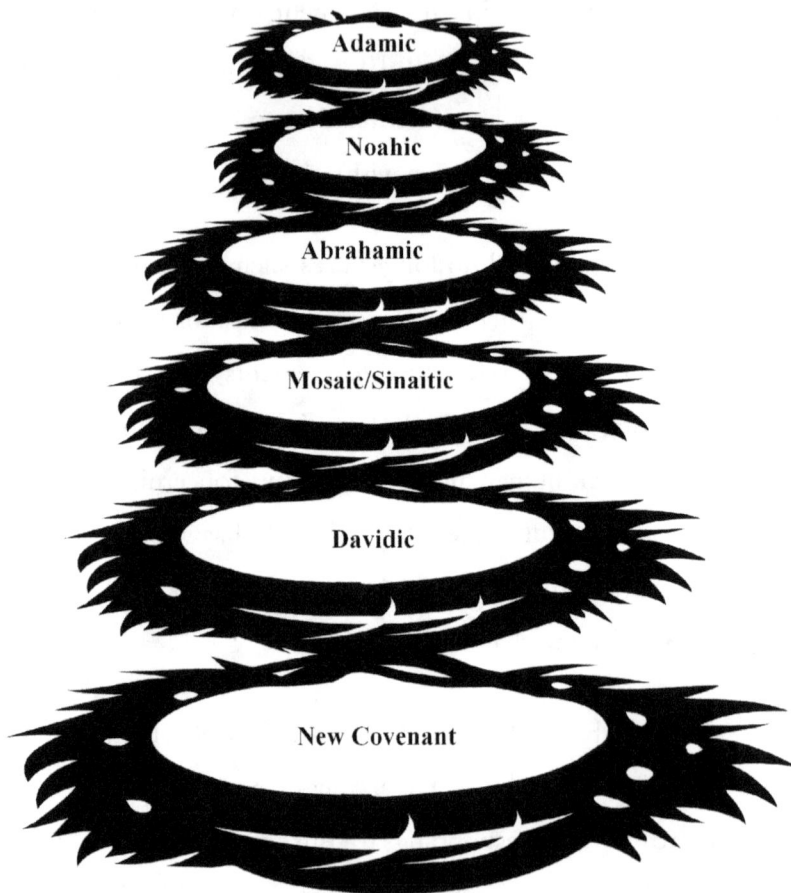

Old Covenants
Nested in
The Love of Jesus
(New Covenant)

Christ offered the ultimate covenant of love to fulfill the covenantal requirements of the previous agreements between God and humankind in what He called a New Covenant (see Hebrews 8:8 and 13). Christianity, therefore, uses love as the basis for resolving societal issues. Love is an ethical truth which is not just internal to the Christian society. Love is an ethical view that transcends (goes beyond) societal environments. Love is the basic element of Christianity. Christianity, then, is an excellent foundation for building a worldview for resolving societal issues.

Conclusion

The information presented in this chapter has been collected and evaluated in a scientific manner. I know it has been boring at times, but sometimes boring is necessary. Gaining knowledge is not always exciting, but it is always appropriate. We must take time to sift through all the information we have, if we are going to get to the facts–if we are going to get understanding. We don't have knowledge until we understand the facts we have accumulated (gathered). We don't become any wiser with just obtaining information. We become wiser when we understand the information we have obtained. Proverbs 4:7 says, "Wisdom is the principal thing; therefore get wisdom: and with all thy getting get understanding."

Geisler and Bocchino make a very important observation about knowledge. They reference Aristotle in noting,

Every field of knowledge begins with certain truths he [Aristotle] referred to as *first principles*. First principles are not conclusions found at the end of a set of premises, but rather premises from which conclusions are drawn. They are axioms -- self-evident truths.[15] (Brackets added.)

The results found here are based on self-evident truths. In all three critical elements addressed (moral values, origin of life, and dealing with societal issues), Christianity is the only worldview whose basis withstands scrutiny. The knowledge of God is all that stays constant. Whether viewed scientifically, philosophically, or faithfully, Christianity is a worldview with a foundation that does not falter. It is a solid worldview because no fault can be found in its core values.

This brings us to the next topic of discussion: How presuppositions (assumptions or beliefs) and principles (core values) help form our worldviews. But, before delving into that subject, we need to discuss Darwinism a little more. This belief system seems to get most of the attention in academia, and you need to have a clear understanding of some misleading notions which accompany it.

5 REPROVING THE KNOWLEDGE OF MAN

"…if your theory is found to be against the Second Law of Thermodynamics, I can give you no hope; there is nothing for it but to collapse in deepest humiliation." (Sir Arthur Eddington)

Deeper Into Darwinism: Biased Beginning

In the last chapter, we discussed how some theories try to make their way into our worldview and replace knowledge of God with humankind's knowledge. We discussed how three critical components within these belief systems (derived from those theories) actually shape a person's worldview. One of those components was one's beliefs about the origin of life (how life began). In that discussion, we examined the Darwinist theory of evolution (or Darwinism). We're going to discuss this theory a little more. The reason we need to do this is because it is perhaps the most propagated (publicized) of the least proven theories in the science class.

In science, a proven theory is called a scientific law because there aren't really any more arguments against a proven theory. Someone (or a group of some ones) has gone through the scientific process of removing all doubt. Until then, it's still simply a theory, which is really an unproven belief in any other environment. However, in science theories are generally accepted as believable, until numerous arguments are accumulated against them. Hypotheses in science are those beliefs which can be argued for or against, so they aren't really held in high regard as are theories. I would label those: less proven theories. They are (in my opinion) theories that may not have many arguments in their favor, but they don't have many against them either.

When I attempt to determine to which of the three categories of scientific belief Darwinism belongs (law, theory or hypothesis), I would say it belongs in the less proven category–hypothesis. In fact, I would probably add a least proven category. What I mean by least proven is that some theories have less data in support of them than data against them. We can label the theory of evolution as one of the least proven because it is formed on hypotheses (assumptions) which have been discussed for decades, but it has not gained any arguments in its favor. In fact, it has lost some of the favorable arguments it had at its inception (beginning).

Darwinism has failed the scientific process of proof testing. It has not only failed the scientific process of proof testing, but it has also failed in the area of common philosophical reasoning (plain old common sense). There are many facts against some of Darwin's assumptions. Yet, this least proven theory still gets a great deal of attention in most public school science classes. It's hard to explain why this is so, because when theories have several arguments against them they are no longer believable. Yet, Darwinism is still presented as a viable (practical) theory. Let's talk about Darwinism a little more. This shouldn't be too boring, but just in case, grab another Dew®.

Darwinism has at least four basic argumentative points upon which it builds its theory (four ways it claims to be credible). The first point involves embryonic recapitulation (pronounced re'-kə-pi-chə-lā-shən). Try saying that five times fast. Wipe the book off when you're done, please. The second argumentative point involves paleontology. The third point purports (suggests) that evolution has not stopped occurring. The fourth point claims certain races are, by nature, superior to others and only they will survive natural selection and live on to improve the continually evolving human race. We'll take a closer look at each of those basic points and demonstrate how Darwinism as a whole is a self-defeating theory–it proves itself false.

One Percent Myth

Encapsulated within those arguments (buried within those points) is the 1% myth. The following excerpt (quote) is from an internet post on the www.boundless.org web site written by Mr. Slater, the site's editor:

For decades the common understanding was that humans and chimps had 99 percent of their DNA in common. Darwinists used this "fact" to support their contention that humans and chimps obviously, therefore, share a common ancestor.

Over the past couple of years, this "fact" has increasingly been shown to be utterly false. According to an article in last month's Science Magazine [June 2007], there's more than a 6 percent difference. A 17.4 percent difference was found in genes expressed in the cerebral cortex [the largest part of the brain, responsible for thought, reasoning, memory, sensation, and voluntary movement]. Museums and textbooks and Web sites continue to regurgitate [state over and over] this 1 percent figure, just as many of them continue to promote Embryonic Recapitulation. But now we know better.[1] (Brackets added for clarification.)

Re-captivated by Recapitulation

The first claim, embryonic recapitulation is probably the most outrageous of all the argumentative points of Darwinism. It is so implausible (unbelievable, doubtful), in fact, that it is generally no longer accepted among even Darwinist advocates (those who promote Darwinism or claim it to be truth). According to Merriam-Webster, recapitulation is

> The hypothetical occurrence in an individual organism's development of successive stages resembling the series of ancestral types from which it has descended so that the ontogeny of the individual retraces the phylogeny of its group.[2]

Dazzled by Drawings

There's a group of words you don't use every day. What Merriam-Webster is saying is the developmental stages of embryos parallel and summarize a species' entire evolutionary development. In plainer English, Darwinist theory claims the development of the embryo is a smaller version of what happens in evolution as a whole.

They based this assertion (claim) on drawings presented by Ernst Heinrich Philipp August Haeckel, a German biologist, naturalist, philosopher, physician, professor and artist. Not only does this guy have too many titles, but he has way too many names. I sure hope he had a nickname growing up. Haeckel claimed embryos from different animals are virtually the same at their beginning developmental stages.

They eventually (according to Haeckel) morph (transform) into the various animal types. His claim was this is an exact representation of what takes place in evolution over a longer period of time. Everything started out looking basically the same, then morphed into the different species we now have.

Haeckel's drawings supposedly included the embryos of a human, hog, calf, rabbit, fish, salamander (a lizard-looking amphibian for those of you who don't get out much), tortoise (looks like a turtle–races the rabbit and wins), and chicken. The drawings depicted (showed) three stages of growth in the earliest portion of the embryos' life cycle. At stage one, the images portrayed a remarkable resemblance in each embryo. In fact, the general formations were almost identical. The only differences in the embryos' build were the thickness of their bodies and the curvature and length of their 'tails'. The second stage characterized substantial changes in the embryonic development of the fish and salamander, but the other embryos still each maintained a great deal of similarity. (All but the fish and salamander still looked almost identical.) It is only at the third stage that the drawings exhibited (showed) a considerable difference in the appearance of the various embryos.

Disowned by Their Own

We already know the idea of embryonic recapitulation is no longer accepted as fact or even theory by most biologists. This includes those who still cling to the hopes of one day proving some aspect of evolution and the Darwinist theories surrounding it. Stephen Jay Gould

(1941-2002) was a paleontologist, evolutionary biologist (a biologist who believes in evolution) and historian of science. Only three titles this time. Haeckel probably would have called him lazy. Not really. Gould was a professor at Harvard University and was highly involved with the American Museum of Natural History in New York. Gould demonstrated embryonic recapitulation is no longer accepted by science as depicted in an article he wrote for *Natural History* magazine:

> We should... not be surprised that Haeckel's drawings entered nineteenth century textbooks. But we do, I think, have the right to be astonished and ashamed by the century of mindless recycling that has led to the persistence of these drawings in a large number, if not a majority, of modern textbooks.[3]

Now, this is from a guy who believed in evolution until the end.

Still Spreading

Gould's article verifies that scientists know the idea of those embryos looking the same at their early stages is ridiculous. In fact, he states that any textbook printed after 1899 should not have these drawings in it. He said it was embarrassing how they continued to do so. Yet, some textbooks still unrelentingly published and promoted this theory as scientific truth; even after such a strong statement by a scientist dedicated to the end of his life in proving the evolutionary theory.

Dr. John G. West and Casey Luskin wrote an article for Discovery Institute entitled "Hoax of Dodos". The article exposed the propagandist (those who put out false information to support their cause) practice of evolutionists to continue promoting fictional information as scientific fact long after it has been proven erroneous (untrue). The article examined and critiqued the film, *Flock of Dodos*, produced by Randy Olson. The film claimed the drawings have not been placed in textbooks since the year 1912.

The authors of the article present drawings from four different textbooks used in public and private schools which portray and discuss embryonic recapitulation as if it is scientific fact. The books were published as recently as 2003. Although each book has variations of the entire model, each shows the beginning stage of embryonic recapitulation according to Haeckel's drawings and three of the four books portray all three stages.

The books clearly propagate the information as science (i.e., as proven fact) to countless, unsuspecting young readers. Since the information is offered by well-respected, highly educated writers, there is no reason the students feel they should question the validity of the context (they won't question whether or not the information is true). West and Luskin include an article from the *New York Times* newspaper where one of the textbooks which contained this information was co-authored by (at the time) the head of the National Academy of Sciences, Dr. Bruce Alberts. The authors write:

In an interview, Dr. Alberts said he believed Haeckel's drawings were:

"Overinterpreted," or highly idealized, rather than outright fakes. But he said they would be removed from the fourth edition of the textbook, to appear the end of this year [2001].[4] (Brackets added.)

West and Luskin then reveal an incident in 2003 where textbook publishers were continually attempting to include the drawings, but were forced to stop after they were met with resistance:

As late as 2003, three textbook publishers were still trying to use Haeckel-based drawings in books submitted for review during the biology textbook adoption process in Texas. When Discovery Institute and Texans for Better Science Education brought up this fact, the reaction of Darwinists in Texas was to insist that the textbooks had no factual errors. Only after months of pushing by critics did the publishers finally agree to withdraw the drawings.[5]

The evolutionists agree that this information is completely false, yet some continue to portray it as scientific fact. This would seem harmless to those who rest on the middle ground between creationism (belief in an Intelligent Designer—God) and evolutionism (belief in a universe which happened by chance); but to those of us who side with creation and an Intelligent Designer (God), it creates an unfair advantage for evolutionists. It forces you as a young Christian (who are forbidden to even discuss God as the

Creator in some public places) to be subjected to propaganda (false information) that is passed as the truth.

You have to learn this information and retain its detailed (though fabricated [made up]) format in order to pass examinations which measure how well you understand it. Then, if that's not bad enough, you must be prepared to continue the process to a greater degree at the next level of your academic career. You must remember what you've learned in the previous grades and add more to it in the next grade. This you have to do, while maintaining your own faith in what you clearly believe as the truth (Creation as demonstrated by the Bible) over the propaganda of evolution which has been proven to be false even by its own followers. Some Darwinists are hoping you will just fall in line with it, but don't worry. God is able to keep you from falling! Here's a little encouragement from Jude 1:24-25 (KJV):

24Now unto him that is able to keep you from falling, and to present you faultless before the presence of his glory with exceeding joy, 25To the only wise God our Saviour, be glory and majesty, dominion and power, both now and ever. Amen.

Pale Promises of Paleontology

Paleontology is the second basic argumentative point of Darwinism we'll discuss. In their book, *Unshakable Foundations*, Norman Geisler and Peter Bocchino define paleontology as "the study of life forms existing in prehistoric times as represented by fossil remains of plants, animals, and other organisms."[6] They define a fossil as "a remnant [remains] of an organism from a past geological age, such as an animal skeleton or leaf imprint that is embedded and preserved in the earth's crust."[7] (Brackets added for clarity.) You probably know these definitions better than I do, but I thought I would include them, anyway.

No Show

Darwin believed paleontology would eventually reveal that there was a gradual process in his theory of evolution. He assumed as the years passed by and the scientific techniques advanced, scientists would find more and more fossils which would 'link' earlier species to modern species proving his gradualism theory (evolution through gradual changes in species over long periods of time). The term "missing link" was coined (invented) and became very popular for a while.

Darwin was, however, well aware that discovery of those missing links was not taking place. He was not so fixed on proving his theory that he would ignore this fact in his findings. I mentioned in the last chapter his willingness to share this in his publication, *The Origin of Species*. Here is more he wrote later in Chapter 9 of that same document concerning those missing links:

The main cause, however, of innumerable intermediate links not now occurring everywhere throughout nature depends on the very process of natural selection, through which new varieties continually take the places of and exterminate their parent-forms. But just in proportion as this process of extermination has acted on an enormous scale, so must the number of intermediate varieties, which have formerly existed on the earth, be truly enormous. Why then is not every geological formation and every stratum full of such intermediate links? Geology assuredly does not reveal any such finely graduated organic chain; and this, perhaps, is the *most obvious and gravest objection* which can be urged against my theory.[8] (Emphasis added.)

So, it seems Darwin was true to science when recording data against his own theory, even though many scientists after him continue to hold on to it. He shows in his writings how he admits the likelihood of having been wrong in his theory of evolution. His theory was proving itself false.

Of course, this was not the only weakness Darwin confessed to in his theory of evolution, but it was a very prominent (major) weakness. This was a weakness that even well-known evolutionists (in their scientific realm) have had to recognize as a deadening blow to Darwin's theory. An online library at the University of California Santa Barbara contains an article with some very interesting quotes from some of those scientists.

One item of interest is a statement concerning Stephen Jay Gould (mentioned previously): "Gould honestly admits that the neo-Darwinian synthesis [the belief which began with Darwin] is not supported by the fossil evidence and 'is effectively dead, despite its persistence as textbook orthodoxy [its accepted belief in textbooks]'."[9]

(Brackets added.) They are saying even though the textbooks would like to make us believe evolution is true; scientists know it's false. The document also quotes David Raup, former Curator of Geology at Chicago's Field Museum of Natural History:

> Well, we are now about 120 years after Darwin, and knowledge of the fossil record has been greatly expanded ... ironically, we have even fewer examples of evolutionary transition than we had in Darwin's time. By this I mean that some of the classic cases of Darwinian change in the fossil record, such as the evolution of the horse in North America, have had to be discarded or modified as a result of more detailed information.[10]

After giving several arguments against Darwin's theory of gradualism, Geisler and Bocchino resolve (determine), "The fossil record shows no evidence of transitional fossils and consequently does not accurately describe a large class of observations."[11] Without observable evidence, theories go unproven and cannot be passed as scientific fact. Whether in the classroom or on one of my favorite TV shows ("Myth Busters"), you would have to admit the theory is dead. The myth is busted. Darwin's theory clearly failed in the paleontological area of science. Even the scientists agree to that. They should admit Darwin's theory is dead.

Bad Show

The well-documented paleontological facts against evolution do not stop some scientists from trying to keep folks thinking there is truth in

Darwin's theory, even if they have to use trickery to keep it going. *Science News* magazine printed an article in 2000 written by R. Monastersky titled "All Mixed up over Birds and Dinosaurs." The article reads:

> Red-faced and downhearted, paleontologists are growing convinced that they have been snookered by a bit of fossil fakery from China. The "feathered dinosaur" specimen that they recently unveiled to much fanfare apparently combines the tail of a dinosaur with the body of a bird. 'It's the craziest thing I've ever been involved in my career,' says paleontologist Philip J. Currie of the Royal Tyrrell Museum of Paleontology in Drumheller, Alberta."[12]

According to Science News, two scientists, one from Utah (USA) and another from Beijing (China) announced at a press conference in Washington, DC that they discovered a fossil which was half dinosaur and half bird. "They called it a missing link between birds and dinosaurs," the article stated. After some time, it was discovered by other scientists that the fossil was a hoax. The two halves of the fossil, the top portion of a bird and the lower portion of a dinosaur, had been fused (pasted) together. The article said other scientists criticized both the team of scientists for presenting it as real and the National Geographic Society for unveiling the fossil before it could be verified by the scientific process. Bypassing the scientific process (when making a scientific claim) is like using steroids to make a run at a sports championship. Someone is seeking an unfair advantage.

Forever False Starting

The third Darwinist argumentative point we'll discuss claims evolution has not stopped occurring. Once you think about it, you should see there is really no logical reason for us to debate this point. This point defeats itself before the debate begins. The idea itself is somewhat of an oxymoron (it contradicts itself). To debate that evolution continues to occur before anyone has proven it has even begun is illogical. It simply does not make sense. We shouldn't even entertain this debate, but we will.

Scientifically Silly

Not only does the idea of evolution still occurring fail the logical test, but it also defies the Second Law of Thermodynamics we discussed in chapter four. This law is based on scientific study and has noted how the universe is in a state of increasing entropy. Entropy, again, suggests that systems in nature tend to move toward disorder as they disperse energy. In other words, things break down or wear out with time. The authors of *Unshakable Foundations* use the example of a car's engine and how it consumes fuel to produce energy. Because of the exploding gas and moving parts, it eventually wears out. That's why we have to continually do maintenance on our vehicles and eventually send them off to the junkyard. Well, maybe you haven't had your first vehicle yet, but you understand; I'm sure. Once you get one, you'll understand it better every time you pay for maintenance service. Remember the quote from Sir Arthur Eddington? "…if your theory is found to be against the Second Law of Thermodynamics, I can give you no hope; there is nothing for it but to collapse in deepest humiliation." There is no hope for the theory of evolution. How can some scientists make a claim that everything is continually evolving into something better when their law of thermodynamics proves everything is getting worse? I don't wish to sound redundant (like I'm repeating myself for no reason), but I need to make this point clear. The theory of evolution defies the Second Law of Thermodynamics.

Gaping Hole in Gap Theory

Nonetheless, there are many who argue the continuance of evolution. Even some Christians attempt to reconcile Scripture (make it work together) with Darwinist theory and say maybe God used evolution to do some of His creative work. They believe in what is called the 'gap theory', an idea of an indeterminate (unknown, untold) amount of time between the verses of Genesis 1:1 and 1:2. This amount of time, they believe, could be billions of years. This belief would leave room for Christians to believe evolution once occurred and perhaps still occurs.

Well, a little closer look at the text found in Genesis 1:1-2 will remedy such a fallacy (correct that misunderstanding). First of all, the first word of Genesis 1:2 is "and." The word 'and' is a conjunction in grammatical terms. Conjunctions are words that connect sentences, phrases, clauses or words. If you want to get all academic, Merriam-Webster defines it as, "an uninflected linguistic form that joins together sentences, clauses, phrases, or words." This means it links the two objects (sentences in this case) so you will not read one without considering what the other one has to say.

Back in 1973 (yeah, I know…) the ABC television station began broadcasting these little short cartoon commercials that taught kids how to use correct grammar. (We could only get three channels where I lived, so ABC wasn't hard to find then.) Those commercials were all a part of a series called Schoolhouse Rock. They used catchy tunes and memorable graphics to familiarize kids with proper sentence structure.

There was one commercial called Conjunction Junction. I know many of you weren't there when the originals came out, but maybe you have seen some of the reruns. It showed a train with several box cars. Some were single words, some were clauses and some were phrases. The box cars were lined up, and then the conductor would connect them with conjunctions (and, but, or). At the end, he would take off on the train; but he couldn't move all the box cars until the conjunctions were in place. The cartoon taught kids that when they see a conjunction in the sentence, don't move on until they have read all of it together. The cartoon was a brilliant idea. It showed that sentences with conjunctions are meant to be read as one—with a pause, perhaps, but not with a gap! You can't get the full meaning of the statement until you read both sides of the conjunction. Genesis 1:1-2 can be read with a pause, but there is no gap there!

Since there is no room for a gap, we should read the second sentence along with the first and see it states that when God created the earth, it was "without form and void." The Hebrew word for void used in verse two is reyqam (ray-kawm) and it means empty. So, even if you pause longer than you should between Genesis 1:1 and Genesis 1:2, you're not going to find anything there. Genesis 1:1 and 1:2 go together to clearly let us know God created the earth without anything in it. There was nothing there until He began creating things which are described in the verses that follow in Genesis 1:1 and 1:2.

Some Christians also use the scripture passages found in Psalm 90:4 and 2 Peter 3:8 to claim there may have been time within the days of creation for evolution to take place. Psalm 90:4 reads, "For a thousand years in Your sight are like yesterday when it passes by, or as a watch in the night." 2 Peter 3:8 reads, "But do not let this one fact escape your notice, beloved, that with the Lord one day is like a thousand years, and a thousand years like one day." Those statements have a meaning which pertains to the context in which they are given. In other words, they need to be read within the verses of their respective chapters to get a good understanding of what they mean. They should not be lifted out and placed into the first chapter of Genesis where creation is described. This would take them out of context and drastically change their intended meaning.

John MacArthur, author of *A Battle for the Beginning: Creation, Evolution, and the Bible*, does a good job of successfully refuting the idea that one day of creation (as described in Genesis) for God could have been as a thousand years to us. He gives good Biblical exegesis (explanation) as to why this is unacceptable, offering substantial Scriptural references. His main point is that Genesis clearly describes each day of creation as a twenty-four hour day.

As we go through the ensuing verses (the verses following verses 1 and 2) in the first chapter of Genesis, we can see after each action God takes, the sun sets, then it rises again to signify the completion of a twenty-four hour day. After God created day and night, we read in verse 5, "And there was evening and there was morning, one day." After God created the atmosphere, we read in verse 8, "And there was evening and there was morning, a second day." We see the same pattern in verse 13, in verse 19, in verse 23, and in verse 31. In six twenty-four hour days, God created everything.

In his argument against the Gap Theory, MacArthur also uses the Bible explanation of how plant life came about and the scientific explanation of how plant life cannot produce (evolve into) animal life. He explains that inanimate objects (like a grain of dirt) can't evolve into a plant or animal. He stresses this point with quotes and an explanation from biochemist Michael Behe:

Evolution can deal only with 'systems that are already working.' By definition, that which does not function simply cannot 'evolve.' It is therefore impossible for inanimate matter to produce biological systems by 'evolution.' Before any evolution can occur, some type of living organism would first have to be produced directly and immediately.[13]

Behe is saying non-living material cannot evolve into a living thing. If "the earth was without form and void [empty]"[14] (Brackets added.) as the Bible says in Genesis 1:2, there is no way the dirt and water God created in Genesis 1:1 could have mutated into some living organisms.

Now, there are some who feel if science proves the Bible to be true rather than false then why is it paleontology has produced fossils which are presumably several million years old, yet the Bible doesn't date life back that far. Some also question why dinosaurs are not mentioned in the Bible, but clearly Paleontology has produced fossils of huge animal life forms. These questions would not cause alarm to the believer in God because we realize that we don't know how God did all He did and we are fine with that. 1 Corinthians 13:12 states, "For now we see in a mirror dimly, but then face to face; now I know in part, but then I will know fully just as I also have been fully known." We understand we can't explain it all, now, but one day God will reveal it. So, we're okay with not explaining those questions. However, we need to address them for the sake of those who are not confident in what the Bible tells us, so we don't appear to be intellectually dishonest in this area.

Well, in response to the first question, God created the earth and all therein at the fully mature state. This is not my philosophical assumption. We can ascertain it truth (discover) by just reading the

Bible. He did not create an embryo and name it Adam and let it grow into the first man. He didn't create an acorn and let it grow into the first oak tree. He created them at the fully mature state. So, if you saw them on the first day of creation, they would have easily appeared to be many years old. The earth itself would have appeared to be many years, possibly millions of years old. So, radiocarbon dating and other forms of determining how old things are may seem accurate from a scientific viewpoint, but they may not tell the whole story. They don't factor in the aged appearance of things at the time of creation.

The other question asks why dinosaurs aren't mentioned in the Bible. Well, there is an interesting passage of Scripture in the book of Job that many theologians feel references dinosaurs. The scripture passage is Job 40:15-24. Read it when you have a chance. The key to this passage is the word "behemoth." Theologians believe the word translates from the Hebrew word *bahemowth* to the English word dinosaur (although *The Brown-Driver-Briggs Hebrew and English Lexicon* states that the exact meaning is unknown). Merriam-Webster defines it as something of monstrous size, power, or appearance." They also say it is "a mighty animal described in Job 40:15-24 as an example of the power of God." I figured if I used the second definition alone, I would be accused of circular reasoning- you know, since I already believe the Bible. But, the first definition Merriam-Webster gives, doesn't reference the Bible and it's still supportive, so maybe that gets us out of the circle. The description for the animal in the text found in Job is certainly that of a huge animal. Although, some believe the animal Job describes could be an elephant or a hippopotamus, *The Brown-Driver-*

Briggs Hebrew and English Lexicon states, "this is patently [obviously] absurd." (Brackets added for clarity.)

We've made a lot of discussion out of a little fact. The fact is that this argumentative point, claiming that evolution never stopped, clearly implodes when viewed objectively or logically. When all the facts are given, it fails on its own. One can't prove evolution never stopped; because no one has ever proven that it began.

Reasoning for Racism: Survival of the Fittest

The fourth and final argumentative point to Darwinism is not just frowned upon by Christians. It is also disapproved of among religious and non-religious groups alike who promote unity and equality among all of humanity. This argument is that nature has designed a process which allows for the 'survival of the fittest'–even among humans. Within this theory lies the idea of some people evolving in a more superior manner than others.

The theory suggests that since those people have evolved superiorly, they will live and continue the human race and all others will die out. This is so the alleged 'weaker race' will not interrupt the perfecting process of nature. Yes, this is the notion which has fueled such atrocities (violent acts) as apartheid (racial separation and discrimination), Nazism (government based on racism), authoritarianism (one person or small group forcing decisions on everyone else), genocide (ethnic cleansing) and other similar enactments which have taken place around the world–even in the United States.

An article in the Washington Post newspaper recounts a study performed by investigative journalist, Edwin Black. Black argued that the Nazi ordeal was a graduated form (bigger movement) of a 'project' exercised in America called the Eugenics Movement. This movement called for what it deemed (considered) inferior citizens (criminals, mentally ill persons, etc.) to be sterilized so as to not reproduce or recycle their inferiority (poor quality) into society. The column states:

Black, whose mother lived under Nazi rule in Poland, writes here with the zeal of an avenger, albeit one with the assistance of 50 researchers who unearthed some 50,000 documents to support his case. He traces eugenics movement back to English economist Thomas Malthus's argument that charitable assistance to the poor 'made no sense in the natural scheme of human progress' and to its later distillation in the theories of Francis J. Galton, cousin and contemporary of Charles Darwin.15

Black explains Galton's level of intellect so readers will know that his suggestions carried clout among the elite (when he spoke, people listened). Galton had a high level of intellect and a positive impact on society: "Galton was no nut; he created the world's first weather maps and later was credited with discovering the uniqueness of human fingerprints."[16] The sterilization project was an attempt to assist nature in its 'survival of the fittest' campaign. Of course, sterilization is not nearly as gross as some things that were done in the Nazi ordeal. The author just wants us to see how the rationale for both falls along the same line.

Some feel it is okay to assist nature in its quest to better humankind by this theoretical 'survival of the fittest' process—even when it means declaring some as 'less fit' and exterminating them. Any person with an ounce of compassion for another human would argue vehemently (very strongly) against such unethical acts against humankind. The idea of 'survival of the fittest' is not centered on compassion, though. It is not based on ethics. It bases its principles (in this case moral values) on evolution, which do not claim to have a Beginner to which it is liable for its actions. It does not admit to have a Modeler by which it should model its moral actions. There should be no surprise, then, that it finds no fault in the results of such ugliness as apartheid, Nazism, and the like.

There are several claims which prevail against this argumentative point of Darwinism (the idea that people continue to evolve into something better through the process of natural selection) beyond the inhumane aspects of it all. Evolutionists still have no scientific proof for their survival of the fittest speculation (based on their submissive agreement to the missing link not offered in paleontology). They have not yet proven that gradualism is making people or animals or plants better equipped to survive in any given environment. They have no scientific proof of evolution in the first place, so they have no excuse for helping evolution along by exterminating undesirables. Just like other 'isms' which argue for superiority (in one race, group, nation, etc.) have no concrete evidence warranting any such theoretical arguments, neither does Darwinism.

If nature could design a model for survival of people, it certainly would not include annihilation of those people in its model. It is logical that nature would intend for one to survive by equally assisting the other. The most logical reason is that nature requires balance. Balance requires harmony. Harmony requires us all–working as equals and living as equals. Darwinism (more specifically the 'survival of the fittest' hypothesis) and any 'ism' (e.g., racism, nationalism, or Nazism) that follows its philosophies are all deadly adversaries to the quest for human equality.

Conclusion

Hebrews 13:9 states, "Do not be carried away by varied and strange teachings; for it is good for the heart to be strengthened by grace, not by foods, through which those who were so occupied were not benefited." The word "foods" here appears to be either the Greek word *phago*, which means consumption or *brosis*, which means corrosion. Either translation fits within this text. We can see that we should not be consumed or corrupted by information that does not benefit us in any way. The arguments for Darwinism just discussed do not benefit humankind. We have objectively determined that.

Darwin's arguments for his theory are very weak; and we have traced its weaknesses (even with its missing links) back to Darwin's own documented skepticism (unbelief). The weaknesses have worsened with the passing of time due to the advancement of scientific study and consequent knowledge (the information gained from that study). To those 'intellectually honest' folks who need scientific proof for the truth, Darwin's arguments greatly lack evidence and are ultimately self-defeating. Those of us who believe the Bible to be true don't even care to debate with Darwin. We know, "For since the creation of the world His [God's] invisible attributes, His eternal power and divine nature have been clearly seen, being understood through what has been made, so that they are without excuse." (Romans 1:20–Brackets added for clarity.) We don't have a use for Darwinist hypotheses (assumptions). This introduces the next subject: the role presuppositions (assumptions) play in determining our worldviews and how we should examine such assumptions before accepting them as truth.

6 EXPOSING THE KNOWLEDGE OF MAN

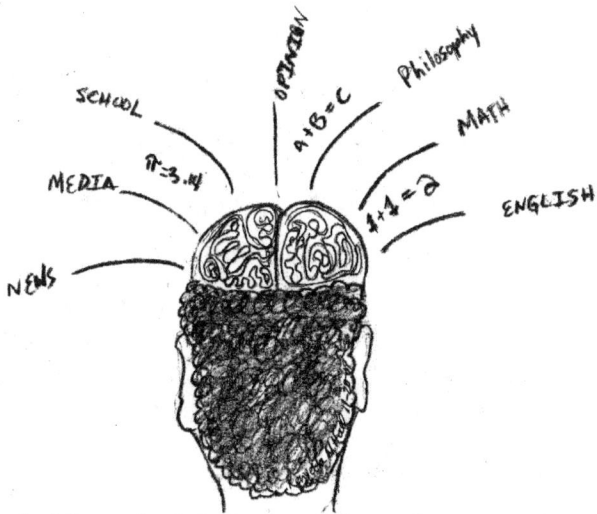

Most of philosophy is influenced through assumptions.

Presuppositions: Feeling Out Philosophy

This chapter discusses the role presuppositions (assumptions) play in how we make decisions on which worldview to accept as our own. This subject is important because most of philosophy (whether taught in high schools, colleges and universities or learned through life's experiences) is influenced through assumptions. Two aspects of presuppositions will be discussed: common knowledge and expert knowledge.

I don't doubt that philosophy is taught in some form at virtually every high school and college or university in the world. I don't have statistics for the entire world, but consider this: In the state of Georgia, every college or university that's a part of the University System of Georgia requires each student to complete twelve semester hours of social science (the discipline to which philosophy belongs) before graduation. Every public high school in Georgia requires three semester hours to graduate. This is according to information on the web sites of the University System of Georgia and the Georgia Department of Education, respectively.

Let's try and estimate how many hours of exposure to new philosophies this means for young students during their high school and college years. A semester is generally sixteen weeks. Classes are offered Monday through Friday so that's five times a week. Class time averages about an hour. Twelve credits at the Associate or Bachelor level in college mean four classes, since you get three credits for each class taken. Three credits in high school would mean three classes, since you get one credit for each class taken there. So, that's a total of seven classes. Seven classes, an hour each, for five days a week, for sixteen weeks would be 560 hours. College courses generally require two to three hours of study outside of class. At least that's what's recommended by experts at www.cliffnotes.com (a website dedicated to preparing students for college). Let's appoint three hours of study for college students (since we know most freshmen try really hard to do their best). Let's assign one hour for high school students. High school students don't study as hard as college students, right? That would give us another 1680 hours for college students and 560 more hours for high schoolers. Based on these numbers (if my math serves me right), that's a rough estimate of 2,800 hours of exposure to some form of philosophy in your latter years of high school and your early years of college. If you spend that much time with anything, you will become quite familiar with it.

I suspect each state within the United States has similar requirements for social science coursework as Georgia, as well as other high schools, colleges and university systems around the world. That means as a young high school or college student, you will be deeply engaged in learning new philosophies for the full portion of your late teen/early adult life. Even if you don't go to college, you will still have to associate yourself with the philosophies of your workplace or the military (if you choose that route). Those philosophies are greatly influenced by those who have graduated from colleges or universities. It is imperative (very important), therefore, to understand the assumptions upon which some of those philosophical systems are built. By the way, this chapter competes with the last chapter for being the most boring; so brace yourself. You might need to switch to Pepsi[®] -- Max.

Contemplating Common Knowledge

The first aspect (characteristic) of presuppositions we will discuss is common knowledge. As for an 'official' definition of common knowledge, you can find one on the web page of Stanford University's Encyclopedia of Philosophy. The definition is buried (and when I say buried, I mean deep) in the statement,

Common knowledge is a phenomenon which underwrites much of social life. In order to communicate or otherwise coordinate their behavior successfully, individuals typically require mutual or common understandings or background knowledge. Indeed, if a particular interaction results in "failure", the usual explanation for this is that the agents involved did not have the common knowledge that would have resulted in success.[1]

That's just way too long and it's hard to follow–mainly because it seems to go in circles. Look at it. It defines common knowledge with the words "common knowledge" embedded in the definition–twice! In the computer programming world, they call that an infinite loop. It just wraps back onto itself and doesn't take you anywhere.

You might not get too far trying to understand that one. So, it might be more beneficial to define the two words individually. *Funk and Wagner's Standard College Dictionary* (Funk and Wagner) defines common as, "pertaining to the entire community."[2] I bet you didn't even notice I switched dictionaries–tricky, huh? Funk and Wagner define knowledge as, "acquaintance with or understanding of a science, art, or technique."[3] If we put those definitions side by side, we can define 'common knowledge' as <u>an acquaintance or understanding held by a community as a truth</u>. A more user friendly definition might be: <u>information that most everyone within a community believes to be true</u>. We'll use this simplified/combined definition for the rest of our discussion on common knowledge. You have the Pepsi Max® ready, right?

Revealing Rogerianism

A well-known philosophy centered on common knowledge is Rogerianism. Okay, it's well-known among those who follow philosophies. It's a form of humanistic (rejects belief in God) psychology involving the fundamental philosophy of common knowledge.

It was developed by Carl Rogers back in 1951. He was working at the University of Chicago at the time. Rogers called this form of psychology, "Client-Centered Therapy." It is based on his belief that each person has the power within themselves to obtain healing of psychological ailments (mental issues) with knowledge common to everybody. The theory behind it was in complete contrast to Freud's and Skinner's ideology that common persons could not help themselves psychologically. Freud and Skinner felt one needs an 'expert' to assist them back to mental normalcy (a healthy mental state). We'll talk about them later, but right now let's hang out in Mr. Rogers' neighborhood.

David J. Murray, one-time Professor of Psychology at Queen's University in Kingston, Ontario (Canada), considers Carl Rogers an important forerunner in client-centered therapy. Again, in client-centered therapy the person needing help is encouraged to 'fix' themselves). According to Murray, this therapy "helps the patient in his or her search for self-respect and self-regard."[4] Murray also insists that Rogers did much to demonstrate the effectiveness of this theory through the scientific method. He references two of Rogers' works–*Client-Centered Therapy* (1951) and *The Therapeutic Relationship and Its Impact* (1967)–as evidence. You're probably looking at those dates, and saying, "Man! That was a long time ago." Some of us don't think so, okay.

Paul Abramson, editor of www.creationism.org and chair of the Biblical Creation Apologetics program at Master's International School of Divinity in Evansville, Indiana, does not appear to praise Rogers' work as does Murray. Abramson gets a little personal as he criticizes Rogers for renouncing Christianity as Rogers went to study psychology at Columbia University. This looks like another case where someone felt they needed to leave pursuit of the Christian faith to be intellectually honest. Abramson claims Rogers would eventually turn to occult activity including necromancy (communication with the dead through some channel). That's scary!

Abramson's personal conviction of Rogers doesn't really matter in his findings. They are more of a personal attack and have nothing to do with debating Rogers' theory. We've been purely objective up to this point and we'll follow along that path. So, we won't join Abramson in his allegations, but he does offer some information that's useful for our discussion.

From a more professional perspective, Abramson saw Rogers' client-centered approach as radical individualism (selfishness). He also felt Rogers' non-directive and non-judgmental counseling approach did not allow for any absolute ethical norms. In other words, there was no accountability in Rogers' method. This falls into the realm of (in line with) Kohlberg's theory of 'epistemologically superior logical operation' we discussed in chapter four. I bet you thought you'd never see that term again, huh? For this reason, Abramson stated, "Rogerianism and related concepts in education today have contributed much to the breakdown of authority and discipline in our homes and schools."[5]

If we fast forward pass a lot of classroom jargon offered by Abramson, you can see the point of discussing philosophical theories surrounding common knowledge. This belief system attempts to nullify (cancel out) belief systems that say there is a need for authority and discipline in any given community. To understand why Abramson feels Rogerianism has caused such poor relational aptitude (ability to grow in good relationships) and lack of respect in our youth (don't you hate getting picked on), we need to do a quick study of the principles behind Rogerianism and other humanistic philosophies.

Humanistic philosophy or Humanism, by the way, claims that humankind doesn't need an authoritative figure (God, parents, police, government–nobody) over it to discipline it into making good moral decisions or having good moral values. Humankind, according to Humanism, can account for good moral values internally. Okay, I won't use that long term again, but you know I was about to. Let me just abbreviate it: E.S.L.O.

Effect on Ethics

Thomas Hardy Leahy, Professor of Psychology at Virginia Commonwealth University, reveals some of those humanistic beliefs in his book, *A History of Psychology: Main Currents in Psychological Thought*. In one instance Leahy discusses how Rogers' humanistic psychology conveys the idea that decent manners, politeness and such are detrimental to personal psychological health. Humanistic psychologists feel it's bad to be polite? Wow!

Leahy mentions how Abraham Maslow, whom he considers a cofounder of humanistic psychology alongside Rogers, openly denounces (speaks against) politeness as a "usual kind of phoniness we all engage in."[6] He then shows how Rogers exerts his belief (makes it known) that displaying decent manners is unacceptable behavior.

Leahy writes:

Rogers (1968) closed an article on "Interpersonal Relationships: USA 2000" by quoting "the new student morality" as propounded at Antioch College: [We deny] "that non-affective modes of human intercourse, mediated by decency of manners, constitute an acceptable pattern of human relations.[7]

Here, Rogers clearly suggests that good manners have a negative effect on human relationships.

Leahy is definitely *not* an advocate (supporter) of humanistic psychology. This is evident in his book. The section which describes the components of this psychology is titled "The Conspiracy of Naturalism." We know (or we should know) anything that involves conspiracy does not involve the scientific method. But, Murray (mentioned earlier) claimed Rogers demonstrated the use of the scientific method in his development of humanistic psychology. Leahy totally disagrees. He writes concerning the aforementioned cofounders of humanistic psychology (Maslow and Rogers):

Humanistic psychologists, including Maslow and Rogers, always counted themselves scientists, ignoring the deep conflict between science's commitment to natural law and determinism and their own commitment to the primacy of human purpose. Humanistic psychology is therefore a sort of fraud trading on the good name of science to push ideas entirely at variance [in disagreement; inconsistent] with modern science.[8] (Brackets added.)

Since humanistic psychology is apparently not built on scientific knowledge, it has been built primarily on common knowledge. One does not use the scientific method to acquire common knowledge. Information gathered as common knowledge is rather 'commonly' accepted as fact or truth. There is no apparent need to systematically develop theories around common knowledge and then test for plausibility or for factuality (to see if the theories hold true). Common knowledge is acceptable for sharing if you are just offering your belief or opinion on something. It is not okay to be passed along as if it is scientific fact.

Since Rogerianism is based upon common knowledge, we can determine its major presupposition is the assumption that it is a psychology of science. It is clearly, however, a psychology of opinion, which has been passed along as fact. That's not being intellectually honesty, now, is it?

Assumptions are All Good–NOT!

Jay E. Adams, author of *The Christian Counselor's Manual* also feels Rogers' system centers on the idea that we have within us the knowledge and resources to correct any mental ailments we may encounter. Rogers' reasoning, as Adams puts it, is that he believes humankind is good at its core; not evil. Rogerianism asserts, Adams says, "Persons with unresolved problems simply have not been living up to their own potential."[9] Adams then explains the Client-Centered Therapy as such:

Adequate resources are there, built in. The task is to plug these in; to release the power. The therapist (or counselor) shares time with a client in order to help him to help himself. The therapist is a catalyst. He assists him much as a midwife does (to use B.F. Skinner's figure) to deliver the solution. The counselee, by the process, is able to come up with the answers himself. Since the resources to solve problems are there in the counselee, there is no necessity for expert advice from the outside.[10]

The key presupposition here is that Rogers believes (or as Adams states, "assumes") humankind is good at the core, rather than evil. The authors, Anderson, Zuehlke and Zuehlke, explain how Rogers claims this is all proven through science, but then the authors expose how he uses a variation of the definition of science. In a discussion on the ideologies (beliefs) of rationalism and naturalism (components of humanistic psychology) held by Rogers, Maslow and others, the authors write,

The good is defined in terms of what is good for the individual (self-centeredness). Humanists believe that their psychology is superior in explaining why people act the way they do, because it is "scientific." For example, Carl Rogers states that true science explores the private worlds of "inner personal meanings." He suggests a redefinition of science that omits the standard scientific method: repeatable, observable, structured phenomena in the objective world.[11]

Again, there is no scientific support at the core of Rogerianism; therefore it is built on presupposition (assumption) rather than scientific fact. Rogers says he uses science to come to his concluded facts, but he doesn't. So, he does not have any facts–only assumptions.

Out with Authority

Claiming that Rogerianism is built upon scientific fact (when it is not) is a critical blow to its credibility, but there is a bigger issue there– at least from a Christian's perspective. Rogerianism claims nothing from outside of a person can assist them in correcting behavioral problems. Adams said that Rogers claims "No authoritative Standard from the outside may be imposed on the counselee. No authoritative 'Word' may be spoken by the counselor as a representative of the Framer of that Standard."[12]   Basically, Rogerianism believes a person's only help for making morally good decisions comes from within.

Therefore, according to Rogerianism, no outside authority, including any Devine Entity (i.e., God), has the power to help a person make morally sound decisions. Rogers' renunciation of Christianity has already been discussed, so we can deduce (determine) that Adams' proper use of "Word" and "Standard" (they are capitalized) refers to God's Word and God's standards.

Pay attention for a minute, now. We're about to make sense of all this. We've determined that Rogers does not use true science as the standard in his theory development. It has been demonstrated how he does not use Biblical principles as the standard. We can raise the question, then, "By what standard (or authority) does he enact his theory during his Client-Centered sessions?" He has to somehow impose *his* beliefs on his clients if he is to stimulate their own inner power to heal themselves. That means he's using *his* standard. That would make *him* the authority. However, he clearly states there can be no outside authority. His practice contradicts the basic element of his principle: no authoritative standard outside of the individual may be imposed upon them. We've stumbled onto one of our old familiar terms. The Law of Non-contradiction has been broken, again. This is why Leahy can accurately label Rogerianism a "fraud." Well, fraud might be a strong word; but Rogers' brand of psychology is certainly not formulated through the scientific process.

To be fair in this discussion, I should state that there are experts who feel some elements of Rogerian psychology (more specifically common knowledge) might be acceptable to and usable by other belief systems, including Christianity, if they are carefully evaluated. This should be the case with any philosophy that has been evaluated from an objective view. Somewhere along the way, some of their basic principles will coincide (agree) with other philosophies, since philosophy, according to Merriam-Webster, is built on humankind's most basic beliefs, concepts, and attitudes. Humans tend to resemble each other in their most basic beliefs, concepts and attitudes–a.k.a human nature.

Adams writes without bias as he views some of the concepts used in Rogers' Client-Centered Therapy: "There is an element of truth reflected by what Rogers does."[13] Adams feels the element of truth in Rogerianism centers around Rogers' disagreement with the idea that only an elite group of humans hold expert knowledge required by others to work out internal psychological problems. In other words, Rogers' theory argues that no individual or group can claim the right to psychological supremacy over other individuals or groups. That would be Gnosticism–thinking you're the only one who has the power or answer to help others. We've covered that.

Anti-Gnosticism is an idea which transcends philosophical differences. In other words, it makes sense within Rogers' system and within other systems as well. That doesn't mean there are two opposing truths supporting the same argumentative statement. There is no such thing. We've covered that as well. That means it is a truth which stays constant. All truth stays constant, regardless of which angle we view it from.

Enough with Gnosticism; there are two prominent (important) presuppositions of Rogerianism which weigh greatly in determining if it can be useful in the Christian worldview. They are the ideas that humankind is inherently good and that no outside authority can help it. We really need to consider the implications of those presuppositions before wholly employing Rogerianism in our Christian worldview. We need to be really careful before we decide to make use of this psychology as a whole.

The first of the two beliefs (humans are inherently good) contradicts badly with Scripture. The Christian would have to compromise their principles to make use of it. The Bible is clear on its presentation of the nature of humankind. As we discussed before (mainly in chapter three), Jesus is recorded on several occasions in stating that the basic nature of humankind is not good. It would defy the Law of Non-contradiction (that again), then, for a Christian to integrate this principle of Rogerianism into his or her worldview.

The second of the beliefs (humankind can't be helped by outside authority) badly contradicts the principles of Theism under which Christianity falls. Theism, again, believes one God made the world and can intervene in its affairs. The idea that humankind can or must depend on its own knowledge and resources for self-sufficiency gives credence to the idea of humans as gods. This is a principle of Pantheism (the belief that all is God or manifestations of God) rather than theism. Again, it would defy the Law of Non-contradiction for a Christian to integrate this principle of Rogerianism into their belief system. I tell you–you're really going to understand this Law of Non-contradiction by the time you finish reading this book.

Let me sidetrack again and offer you a full understanding of the danger of holding to this theory that humankind is inherently good. I want to take a moment to really illustrate the danger of believing a person can move towards better decision-making by themselves or if I may use my preaching voice: the danger of progressing to the nth *degree of sin*.

I remember first learning about variables in math from Mr. Cutchens in Algebra I. He took his time and taught us the concept of variables. I was young then and so I couldn't really see where I would ever need to know the concept of variables for the math in my every day activities. I am much older now and I think I'm a little wiser and I still don't see a need for knowing the concept of variables for performing my normal math routines. I know there might be some engineers out there that beg to differ that variables in math are quite useful, but I'm talking about for my own personal use.

Mr. Cutchens kept it simple when he taught us the concept of variables. He used binomials where you have only two terms (you know, something times something = some number). He taught us that variables are letters that take the place of unknown numbers in an equation. He always used x and y in his examples as in X times Y = some number. He told us the value of a variable may change depending on the scope of the problem. Until the problem is fully realized (solved), the variable is unknown. He would give us the value for one variable then after we understood the concept, we could figure out the value for the other variable.

Once I got the concept of variables, I thought they were pretty cool. I still thought they were useless, but it was fun to work out the problems–until Mr. Cutchens started throwing in exponents. When he taught the concept of exponents, the letter he used for the exponent variable was always the letter "n." Exponents can be tricky, because they make the numbers grow much faster. You can have just one number with an exponent and that one number can get big in a hurry.

I'm sure most of you know this, but work with me for a minute. If you see a variable exponent beside your number, it means you have to multiply the number by itself however many times the variable stands for. So if that n=4 and you have 10 to the nth power (or nth degree), then you multiply 10 by itself, four times. So you multiply 10 x 10, then multiply whatever that equals by 10, then multiply that by 10 again, which is ten thousand. $10^4 = 10,000$.

You can see when the variable is in the exponent position your numbers can grow really big really fast can't they? It's called growing exponentially. When your number is growing to the nth degree, it can get out of control really quick. Just think if you have an exponent where n=10. 10 to the 10th degree equals 10,000,000,000 (ten billion). See how quickly the numbers can grow when they're exponential? And we're just using the nice round number of 10. Imagine if our number was 437 and our n=24. 437^{24}. You'll run off the paper trying to solve that one. It could get out of control real quick, couldn't it? That's how exponents work in math.

Once I understood the concept of exponents and variables, I was ready to take on the world of algebra. I enjoyed working out binomial and trinomial equations where I had to solve for the variables, even if they included exponent variables. I still, however, felt like the concept of variable exponents were of no use beyond the classroom. I spent all of my childhood and most of my adult life feeling that way. In fact, it was not until very recently that I finally realized a use for understanding the concept of variable exponents and that use had nothing to do with math.

I was talking once with one of the Missionaries at our church and we began to casually address the concern with prominent pastors where currently making the news headlines for the wrong reasons. Our discussion went from how terrible things they were "allegedly" doing were to how could someone so high (in the religious ranks) stoop so low. I thought about that long after our conversation was over. I concluded that they just started with small wrongdoings and eventually it got way out of control.

Then, somewhere along the way of my pondering this thing, it hit me. Here is a very logical use of math's concept of variables. This concept explains the danger of playing around with sin. The variables associated with sin are always in the exponent position. Sin always grows to the nth degree. It grows exponentially. And we just saw when something grows to the nth degree it can get really big really quick. It can easily get out of control. Maybe (if the accusations were true) those pastors didn't realize the concept of exponent variables as it relates doing wrong.

Let's look at sin at the nth degree for a few minutes. I want to show you how this thing can get out of control quickly. In my opinion (now this is just my opinion). This isn't the result of deep, concentrated theological study. I just made this up; but it makes sense. And, it aligns well with Scripture.

In my opinion, there are four exponential variables of sin and they all just happen to begin with the letter 'n'. There is the "no way" variable. There is the "nonchalant" variable. There is the "no big deal" variable. And finally, there's the "nothing bothers you anymore" variable. Now pay close attention to these variables in all of this.

Here's how I think these variables work:

When we are in the right relationship with God (when we are really allowing the Holy Spirit to reign over our lives), I don't care what kind of sin comes our way, we're going to say "No way! I'm not doing that! I'm not saying that! I'm not watching that! I don't want to hear that!" At this point, we see sin as a "no way" variable. Regardless of what the wrong is, we're just not doing it. We're so focused on doing what's right according to God's word that people can do whatever they want to try to tempt us, but we will hold our ground. That's when we're fully in tune with the Spirit of Christ that dwells within us. Don't you wish we could all just stay right there?

Well, sometimes we get a little relaxed with this idea of sin. Sometimes we'll place the nonchalant variable in the sin equation. We expose ourselves to bad situations. We may not physically take part in any wrongdoings, but sometimes just too much exposure will give us a nonchalant view of sin. It may just be the type of movies we watch or the video games we play or the books we read or even the conversations we join in on. If we hold that nonchalant view too long, it will grow quickly. And before you know it you're at the no big deal variable.

When the variable reaches no big deal, we have let bad behavior become commonplace in our lives. We've become desensitized to it. At this point, we'll not want to just watch what's going on or listen to what's being said, anymore. We'll want to take an active part in it. And we will, because at this point, it's no big deal to us.

Sin at the degree of "no big deal" will still bother our conscience, but not enough to make us stop. It'll just make us want to hide it from those who we know are still seeing sin with the "no way" variable. We'll be careful around other folks, too. Even though we see it as no big deal, we don't want to show them too much.

If we stay at the "no big deal" variable of sin a short while, it won't take long to move to the "nothing bothers me anymore" variable. Why? That's because (as we just saw) exponents get out of hand really quick. Of course at that point, we don't care who hears us or who see us or who knows us. As Mrs. Helen Baylor says in her testimony, we'll do "everything we're big and bad enough to do." If you've never heard Mrs. Baylor's testimony on her *Helen Baylor Live* CD (1999), you should find it on YouTube and listen to it. That's an excellent testimony of why you can't play with sin. She really took it to the nth degree. But as she states in her testimony: she had a praying grandmother and she knew enough to call on the name of Jesus. Man, I love that testimony!

Sin grows too big too fast. If you hang around it too much, even if you're not taking part in it, you will get relaxed with it and eventually go from "no way" to "nonchalant." Then you will casually begin to take part in it, even if it means sneaking to do so. You'll find yourself going from "No way!" to "No big deal." Soon you'll stop hiding it altogether and it won't take long before "Nothing bothers you anymore."

Let me give you a real life example of how quickly sin grows to the nth degree. Now, my testimony is nothing like Mrs. Baylor's, but it will serve the purpose. This story might drift a little, but stay with me. There's a testimony in all this. Revelation 12:11 tells us that people overcome the doing wrong by the words of our testimonies.

When I joined the military, my first order of business was to get my dream car. I told myself as just as soon as I get there, that's what I'm going to do. I will go out and get myself a used-but nice, 1982, two-door, 5-speed --- Toyota Corolla. That was my dream car. I know what you're thinking: a Corolla–a dream car? Hey, that was my dream car. You see, when I was in the eleventh grade; my sister would let me use her '82 Corolla. It was dependable and it got excellent gas mileage. That's just what I needed to go out to the country to see my then girlfriend (now wife). She lived deep into the country.

Now, if I couldn't borrow my sister's '82 Corolla to go out there, then I had to use my Uncle Joe's 60-something Ford Falcon station wagon. He had other cars, but it seems the Falcon was always the one that was available. And he would let me borrow it anytime I wanted to. In fact, Uncle Joe was proud to let me borrow his Falcon to go see my girlfriend. He once dated her aunt. He thought very highly of that family.

Uncle Joe worked in construction all his life. He was a big man and he had a deep voice; but he was just as jolly as one could be. He laughed every time he got ready to say something. He would always chuckle when I asked him to borrow the Falcon to go see my girlfriend. It just tickled him to know that I was going to "court" the niece of one of his girlfriends of the past.

He used to enjoy loaning me that old Falcon and I wasn't ashamed of it, but I'd much rather drive the Corolla. The reason I preferred the Corolla wasn't because of mechanical or maintenance issues. My Uncle kept that car running like a sewing machine. It seemed like he always had brand new tires on it. The inside was pretty clean, too, but he didn't care much about the outside. The paint was faded badly and it had some surface rust, but that didn't bother me. It didn't even bother me when my girlfriend's sister picked at me when I drove up in it. She called it the Monster Mash Mobile. That didn't bother me one bit, though. I was riding and I got to see my girlfriend, so I was happy and blessed.

The only thing that bothered me about that Falcon was the gas mileage. It wasn't nearly as good on gas as the Corolla. All my extra money was going into the tank when I drove that thing over to my girlfriend's house. When I got to drive my sister's Corolla I was able to keep some extra spending money. Needless to say, I fell in love with that Corolla. So, I made up in my mind then: First car I get will be a Corolla. That's how the 1982, two-door, 5-speed Toyota Corolla became my dream car.

I remember getting to California for my first duty station and asking around about car places. I got one of the guys to take me downtown Seaside (a nearby city) a few times to check out the car lots there. Now, this guy had an old Chevy Chevelle. That car was clean. The engine sounded really strong. It had a beautiful sound system and had a nice set of rims on it. It was all tricked out. I thought a little about how that might be a nice car to have, but my mind went back to the '82 Corolla. That was my dream car.

On the first trip to Seaside I didn't find what I wanted, so I kept searching. In the meantime, I was speaking with my brother on the phone one day and he asked me what I was doing at my new duty station. I said, "Nothing much just looking for a car, right now." He said, "Man you ought to get yourself a Mazda RX7. You don't have any bills. All you have to worry about is the car payment and the insurance and you can handle that." I was 18; so, insurance would have probably cost me more than the car. But I didn't think about that. I was thinking about the other thing he said. He said, "Man, that's a chick magnet!" That made me think about it a little bit, "Hmmm, Chicks dig the RX7?" The Mazda RX7 was the hottest sports car for the price back then. I thought about it hard. Then, I said, "Man, I don't need a chick magnet. I have a chick."

Since Seaside didn't produce what I wanted, I went to Salinas (a city further away) looking for the car of my dreams and there she was. I saw it from the down the street. It looked like the only car on the lot. It appeared to have a glow about it, but actually that was just the sun shining off of it. It was white and the sun was bright that day. My buddy pulled into the car lot and we got out and started going over towards it. Some young nice looking female salesperson came up behind us and was walking and talking, following us to the car. As I look back, I figure the manager sent out the young female since we were two young guys. I tell you that devil is the trickiest creature in the garden. Good looking chick trying to talk me into buying something I don't want. She may as well have been a Panda bear speaking Chinese, though. I didn't understand a word she said. I had a made-up mind. No chick-selling chick magnets could change it, either.

I signed the papers, got my Corolla and drove off the lot. I didn't haggle, didn't test drive–nothing. It's just by the grace of God that the car wasn't a piece of junk, because I didn't think to check anything on it. I could have stumbled on a bad deal and wouldn't have known it until it was too late. But that's what Psalm 91:11 means when it says, "For he shall give his angels charge over thee to keep thee..." God must have had angels watching over me then. It turned out that my '82 Corolla was in excellent condition all around.

Needless to say, I became rather popular with a fresh set of wheels. Everybody wanted to ride here; ride there. Pretty soon the guys were inviting me to Los Angeles (LA) for their weekend getaways. One of the people in my platoon was from that area, so almost every weekend they visited LA. At first, I was saying, "NO WAY! I'm not going to LA and hang out all weekend with you guys!" You should have heard those guys around the barracks cursing and fussing and acting foolish. And that's when they were sober. I could just imagine how they got when they were in LA partying all night. And I know they were out all night, because they came back telling their war stories. Some of their reports had my eyes popping out–didn't bother them one bit, though. I was like "No way! Not me!!"

They kept inviting me and pretty soon I got kind of nonchalant with my responses. Instead of saying, "No way," I began to say, "We'll see. Maybe one day." Well, that one day came and I agreed to ride down with them. I hung out with them for a weekend. I kept telling myself, "Well, I won't be cursing and drinking and carrying on. I'll be alright." That's what I kept telling myself. I went along and before you know it I became a regular. I didn't drive my car all the time, but even when I didn't I was the designated driver for our nights out, since I didn't drink. So, I was still of good use to them.

I kept it fairly clean, though. Then one time (and I had driven my dream car this time) I decided I'd try a wine cooler while we were at the club. They had been nagging me for the longest about how it was only 5% alcohol and it was almost like drinking Kool-Aid®. (Remember that statement in chapter two about not drinking the Kool-Aid®? I wish I knew then what I know now.)

After a while I thought, "Five percent–I can handle that." I sipped on one for a while until it was gone. It didn't bother me, so guess what I thought? "No big deal." A little later that night, I got another one and sipped on it. That second one gave me a little buzz. I could tell I was getting intoxicated, because I begin to feel something I had never felt before and it wasn't the Holy Spirit. It was the spirits from the bottle, not the Spirit from the Lord. When we left the club to go back to the guy's house, one of my buddies offered to drive. I said, "Naw, I can handle this."

I was driving down the streets of LA just buzzing along. We were laughing and carrying on and then all of a sudden, "Boom!" My '82 Corolla met up with a 70-something Ford Maverick. It was not a good meeting. Let me explain something about Corollas and Mavericks. '82 Corollas are made of aluminum or something of the sort. Ford Mavericks are made of cold hard steel or something close to it. It wasn't pretty for the Corolla.

None of us were hurt, just shaken up a bit. We got out of the car and all I could smell was alcohol. The guy I ran into was as drunk as a skunk. He jumped out and asked me, "Man what were you thinking? I had the green light." I couldn't think of anything to reply with. I was mad, sad, scared, confused and everything else. Alcohol will really mess with your emotions. I didn't know what to say to him. So, I said, "What were you thinking? I had the green light." To this day, I don't believe either one of us knew who really had the green light.

I guess God was in a good mood that night. I didn't get arrested and didn't get a ticket. I don't know what became of the guy in the Maverick. I know they had to tow my little dream car away. It took about two months for me to get my car back from the body shop.

In the police report it listed a Ford Maverick that I ran into that night. In my mind, it was the hand of God stopping me in my tracks. I was quickly approaching the nth degree of sin. 1 Corinthians 10:13 says that with every temptation, God offers a way of escape. That was a tough way to get me to escape where I was headed, but it got me out of there. I was playing with sin and it was quickly getting out of control. God saw fit to get my attention. And He got it. I realized: you can't play with sin. I took that door of escape and I didn't let the doorknob hit me on the way out.

After that incident, the only other trip I made to LA with those guys was to go pick up my dream car once the shop repaired it. I was back to the "no way" variable when it came to the LA crew. I started going to Chapel on Sundays, instead. I found myself growing back closer to the Lord. Before long they had me teaching children's Sunday school and singing in the choir. I was back where I was supposed to be.

That's my testimony, but every story doesn't end that way. I can tell you a story with one of my best friends as the main character (on those same trips to LA) and it didn't end so well. Somehow, my buddy got nonchalant with his approach to sin. I tried my best to get him to see the dangers of playing with sin, but I couldn't. Before I left there, he was all out with that LA bunch. It placed his life in shambles.

I can say that when we went back to visit 20 years later (glory to God), he had come back to Christ and was living a Godly life again. That's just more proof of Mr. Bisset's research that many who do "leave the faith" find their way back. It was good to see him completely recovered. I didn't judge him, but I couldn't help but wonder to myself a little, "Why didn't he see the way of escape sooner?" I know we're all different. I'm not trying to act like a goody two-shoes or make it seem like my sin was lighter than my friend's. Sin is sin. The only thing that changes is how we view it–either with a no way attitude, a nonchalant attitude, a no big deal attitude or a nothing bothers us about it attitude. My sin was no different than his sin when it came down to our relationship with Christ. We both walked away from a great relationship with God.

The point of the testimony is this: It's very dangerous to expose yourself to sin like that. Sin grows on you very quickly. It grows exponentially. It grows to the nth degree. It's extremely risky to take on the philosophy that Rogers offers and think that people are inherently good and will eventually make better choices on their own. If you remember the discussion in chapter 4 on entropy (the measure of disorder in a system–I sure hope you do), when it comes to our behavior, it closely resembles entropy. We don't get better at making good decision on our own. If we don't have outside assistance steering us to do good, we will get increasing worse at it as time continues to pass.

Okay, I'm done with the sermon – so back to the discussion. There are many principles of common knowledge that were not discussed here. The principles deliberated were used to demonstrate how Rogerianism's common knowledge has underlying presuppositions at its core which are not based on scientific fact. Instead, they are based on information with which its community of holders is familiar. It is evident that Rogerianism as a form of psychology or as a philosophy *is not* obtained through the scientific (i.e., technical, systematic, exact) process, but rather common knowledge. It is therefore mislabeled as a psychological 'science.' It is also evident that some of its principles greatly contrast (differ from) Christian principles. There is enough documented information to assist you in discerning (determining) if Rogerianism as a whole should become a part of your Christian worldview. I'm thinking not.

Exploring Expert Knowledge

Second up for discussion in the roles of presupposition as it relates to choosing a viable worldview is expert knowledge. Let's take a look at two forms of psychology which rely heavily upon expert knowledge (Freudianism and Behaviorism). We'll look over the statements of some well-known folks in the field of psychology who follow those ideologies. We'll also identify some presuppositions associated with this school of thought as we explore how those principles relate to the Christian worldview.

Again, we need to figure out a good definition of expert knowledge. Just as before, we can find a definition on the web page of Stanford University's Encyclopedia of Philosophy. The definition is wrapped up in the statement, *"Techne* is at the most basic level, what can be learned and taught. The word is usually used for a body of professional knowledge, mastered by experts on whom laypeople may safely rely. It is often translated 'art' or 'craft' or 'skill,' but in these pages it will be rendered 'expert knowledge'."[14] Once again, we find ourselves stuck in a loop because the words 'expert knowledge' are used as a part of the definition itself. So, once more we will break down the two words and define them individually. Funk and Wagner defines expert as, "having, involving, or displaying special skill or knowledge derived from training or experience."[15] It defines knowledge the same as before. We wouldn't expect a change there, now, would we? It is the "acquaintance with or understanding of a science, art, or technique."[16] Keeping true to form, we will combine the definitions and define 'expert knowledge' as

<u>teachable, learnable techniques held by formally trained persons, which non-trained persons can rely upon for help</u>.

If we're going to talk about expert knowledge, we have to discuss Sigmund Freud. Freud's work in the field of psychology is well respected among psychologists and professional counselors. We can simply consider the amount of literature available on Freud's work and his contributions to the field and determine his impact. Any library search performed on psychology or psychoanalysis will yield a plethora (a great deal) of writings by or about Freud. In fact, according to Peter D. Kramer, professor at Brown University, Freud is known as the father of psychoanalysis (a form of psychological therapy).

Being Frank with Freudianism

James A. Schellenberg, Professor of Sociology at Indiana State University, states that Freudianism (or psychoanalysis) assumes, "the centrality of unconscious emotional forces, the dynamics of repression and resistance, and the importance of childhood experience."[17] You're probably thinking the same thing I thought when I read that the first time: "Say what?" What he is saying in the basic principle of Freudianism is that your past experiences determine your current mental state–I think. A secondary principle is that with expert knowledge someone can administer psychoanalysis and correct a person's defective mental state (fix what's mentally wrong in a person).

The presupposition attached to those principles is the assumption that Freud gathered expert knowledge required to progress these principles along into theories and ultimately scientific facts. There is copious (a whole lot of) documentation of Freud's questionable practices and nonfactual (false) findings. The jacket to Kramer's book, *Freud Inventor of the Modern Mind* reads,

...but though Freud compared himself to Copernicus and Darwin, his history as a physician is problematic. Historians have determined that Freud often misrepresented the course and outcome of his treatments—so that the facts would match his theories."[18]

Looks like Freud falsified some of his findings. His false information was not the only error in judgment he was known for. Paul C. Vitz, Professor Emeritus of Psychology at New York University, details Freud's extensive cocaine usage (whoa!!!) and his attempt to have the drug accepted as a viable means of cure in the psychoanalytic process. That Siggy was a naughty boy!

Actually, Freud wasn't an intentional drug abuser. He believed the drug had physiologically medicinal properties (he considered it a medicine). He did so until he realized the drug may have had a detrimental effect on one of his friends and colleagues, Ernst Fleischl, to whom he introduced the drug. Vitz writes in *Sigmund Freud's Christian Unconscious*,

Freud got Fleischl to take cocaine, which he thought would cure his friend's morphine addiction and have no undesirable effects of its own... Freud later bitterly acknowledged that he may have hastened his friend's death, saying "it was the result of trying to cast out the devil with Beelzebub."[19] (Beelzebub is another name for the devil. It's like saying he was using evil to combat evil or two wrongs don't make a right.)

That was obviously unintentional and gravely unfortunate on Freud's part; but even a number of Freud's colleagues (experts in his field) disagreed strongly with some of his other *intentional* practices and resulting theories. John Forrester, Professor of Philosophy at the University of Cambridge, wrote a book entitled *Dispatches from the Freud Wars—Psychoanalysis and Its Passions* to document and analyze debates over Freudianism among some psychology professionals. Robert S. Steele's *Freud and Jung Conflicts of Interpretation* and Peter Gay's *Freud a Life for Our Time* both extensively document the disintegration of a relationship between colleagues Sigmund Freud and Carl Jung (another pioneer in the field) due to Jung's belief that Freud was, as Gay writes, "placing personal authority above truth."[20] There is much documented evidence of Freud's non-scientific practices. That forces us to assume that he accumulated expert knowledge in his process, when it is apparent he may not have. You might want to consider this before accepting the entire philosophy of psychoanalysis as a part of your worldview.

Rebuttal of Burrhus' Behaviorism

Hey, wake up. Let's talk about Behaviorism a little. B.F. (Burrhus Frederick) Skinner is also well known in the psychology profession for his contributions in the area of behaviorism. Behaviorism, as Funk and Wagner defines it, is "the theory that the behavior of animals and man is determined by measurable external and internal stimuli acting independently."[21] According to Skinner, "We can analyze a given instance of behavior in its relation to current setting and to antecedent events in the history of the species and of the individual."[22] Yeah, I know–another "Say what?" moment. Similar to Freud's psychoanalysis, behaviorism purports that our past experiences are the driving factor in determining our conduct.

Beyond its similarity to Freud's psychoanalysis, a basic principle behind Skinner's behaviorism is that our conduct can be funneled by affecting certain influences on our environment. Skinner used positive reinforcement (reward) and negative reinforcement (punishment) to prove this basic principle of his theory. You must have heard of this positive and negative reinforcement by now. I'm sure you've even experienced it in action if you have not behaved as you were expected to at times.

Behavioral modification (getting folks to act the way you want them to) is the desired outcome of this practice. Skinner contends that our entire spectrum of functioning can be programmed with the aid of positive or negative reinforcements. In other words, we can make folks do anything we want by doing something good or something bad to them. Skinner's principle maintains that even thinking is a form of behavior, as he declares in his book, *Verbal Behavior*. So, we should be able then to control someone's thought process through positive and negative reinforcement.

The presupposition which stands out most with Skinner's basic principle is we must assume that the observed data used in his scientific methods is a valid representation of all humankind. He often used animals as his subjects. Samples of data taken from the observance of rats and pigeons may prove scientifically true for rats and pigeons, but to say that people will respond to reinforcements the same as rats and pigeons takes a great deal of speculation. We are not animals. The data you gather on animals will not all apply to people. Skinner would have had to have leaned towards speculation to accept the results of his sample data as a valid representation of all available data. In other words, he was guessing that all people will respond to reward and punishment the same as rats and pigeons.

Even stating you can control the thinking of animals is speculative. Take cats for instance. Cats are very creative. Cat owners and trainers can probably give countless stories and presentations of their cats doing really cool stuff. But, do you think a cat can determine within itself something like eating rat meat is not healthy for you because it's high in cholesterol? I don't eat rat meat because I know red meat is high in cholesterol. Okay, I have other issues with eating rat, too, but let's just use that one for now. Try and make a cat understand that meat high in cholesterol is not good for you and see if it works for the cat. If we dice the rat meat up and disguise it, the rat will probably eat it. If it's disguised well enough (and cooked just right) I would probably eat it, too.

Now, you can beat a cat over the head every time it touches a rat and pretty soon it will realize rat meat is bad for you. That's the behavioral enforcement Skinner suggests. You've altered the cat's thought process, right? Wrong. The cat is not thinking rat meat is high in cholesterol and is therefore bad for you. The cat has realized the pattern of events which follows its behavior (in this case–touching the rat). Touch rat. Get hit–bad. Don't touch rat. So, Skinner's theory that thinking is a form of behavior that we can manipulate doesn't really look all that scientific. We haven't made the cat change its way of thinking. All we have done is control the animal behavior of a cat.

You can do the same for humans–beat them into submission. But even if you force the behavior of humans, you don't control their thinking. You just control how they respond to your enforcement. Haven't you seen movies where a certain people were enslaved or strongly controlled by others? Eventually, they would pull together and plot a scheme for freeing themselves. Their thoughts were never under control; it was just that they were forced into a specific behavioral pattern until they could think of a way out of it. That doesn't just happen in the movies. It has happened over and over throughout history.

Skinner's data may have been gathered scientifically, but it wasn't a valid representation of us humans. I say the data *"may* have been gathered scientifically." We're not sure he was truly scientific in his method of collecting that data. Schellenberg states that Skinner was not totally scientific in his collection methods and was indeed speculative (guessing) with his findings. Schellenberg writes in a chapter titled "The Blindness of Masters,"

Being a master of anything tends to carry with it certain single-mindedness of purpose. There is a resolve to forge ahead in whatever is the chosen line of activity... Let us start with Skinner. His approach has often been labeled as one-sided, extreme in what is left out of consideration... in key aspects, then, Skinner's operant psychology systematically excludes or neglects considerations of potential importance.[23]

Schellenberg goes on to discuss how Skinner's justification of rate of behavior and probability did not account for the difference in general behavior and specific behavior. All of that doesn't mean a lot outside of psychology, but it does help us determine if Skinner was truly scientific in his process–apparently not.

With Schellenberg's quote concerning "being a master of anything..." in mind, we might want to also consider some of Skinner's own convictions, before accepting any presuppositions to his expert knowledge. Skinner writes about a fictional work of his, *Walden Two*, which describes his 'scientific' methods and their desired outcome:

I was made aware of a basic issue when *Walden Two* was immediately attacked as a threat to freedom. Its protagonist was said to have manipulated the lives of people and to have made unwarranted use of his own value system. I discussed the issue in a paper called "Freedom and the Control of Men" in 1955 and in a debate with Carl Rogers in 1956… I did indeed argue that people are not in any scientific sense free or responsible for their achievements, but I was concerned with identifying and promoting the conditions under which they feel free.[24] (Emphasis added.)

If you pay close attention to the emphasized (underlined) portion of Skinners quote, you will recognize the following: Skinner admits there is "a basic issue" with his process. He admits to being manipulative with his subjects of study. He also admits he presented findings in a false light. That "intellectual dishonesty" term comes back to mind.

Only the Elite are Allowed

A final discussion on presuppositions of expert knowledge (did I hear cheering?) is the idea that the knowledge can only be held by certain individuals. Expert knowledge claims that there are few who are capable of achieving the level of expertise required in completing a certain task—in this case, psychoanalysis. Most folks are merely relegated (reduced) to being patients. This is the ideology Jay E. Adams explores in The Christian Counselor's Manual. He makes it clear that he feels this way of thinking is incorrect. He points out Freud and Skinner as the main contributors to this mindset. Adams writes concerning expert knowledge,

The first approach is adopted by those who believe that counseling [psychoanalysis to psychologists] can be done only from a point of view of expert knowledge. They hold that counseling must be restricted to some small coterie [exclusive group] or elite group of technocrats. People of this sort develop castes [classes—as in upper class/lower class] and priesthoods (secular or otherwise). To the counseling priesthood alone is assigned the task of counseling. Among the leading theorists of this school are Freud and Skinner.[25] (Brackets added for clarity.)

Adams is very critical of the likes of Freud and Skinner. He discusses pacts (agreements) that professionals in the field of psychiatry make among themselves, which insinuate (hint) they all share the same sentiment (attitude). The common person cannot be helped without expert knowledge. They feel only trained professionals hold the knowledge to help folks. Adams claims they use "esoteric jargon [mysterious language] and institutionalized techniques."[26] (Brackets added.) He even refers to them as Gnostics (a belief that only a few have such knowledge), because they feel only they have the power to counsel others back to mental stability.

Of course, the idea that only a select few possess the ability to counsel others did not begin with Freud and Skinner and the advent (start) of psychoanalysis and behaviorism. This issue of Gnosticism was present as far back as the early church. I suspect it existed much further than that. Millard Erickson discusses Gnosticism in the early church in his book, *Christian Theology*. He writes, "But we must remember that the fourth and fifth-century church was wrestling with problems resulting from '…the rise of Gnostic doctrine…'"[27]

I must say there are cases where Christian counselors feel expert knowledge is required to handle situations that arise within the counseling process. If certain conditions are discovered, they feel, expert help/advice should be sought. The term expert here, though, only signifies a person has been trained above and beyond the average person. It does not suggest they are the only ones who can help that situation.

Dr. Ronald Cobb feels this is the case. Dr. Cobb is another professor at Luther Rice University. I guess by now you think I'm advertising for Luther Rice as much as I use these guys' quotes. It's an excellent school, but I'm only using the information because it's great information. They didn't pay me to advertise for them.

Dr. Cobb writes concerning eating disorders, "As you are aware, this is a life-threatening disorder that may require professional intervention in advanced cases."[28] Dr. Cobb, in lecturing the class on Christian Counseling, was cautioning his students to not try and take on counseling situations for which they were not trained properly. Dr. Cobb doesn't feel every case requires a professional's presence, however. In fact, I have witnessed several lectures he has expounded on (talked in detail about) the effectiveness of lay (non-professional) counseling.

In one of his courses, Dr. Cobb uses as a textbook, *Called to Counsel*, by John R. Cheydleur. This book is purposed to assist laypersons in effective counseling. Another of Dr. Cobb's textbooks of choice, *How to Be a People Helper*, by Gary Collins also makes strong arguments that lay counseling is just as effective as professional counseling in many cases.

Collins does an excellent job of illuming (pointing out) the positive effects of laypersons in the area of what he calls "people helping." He does not discredit the works and efforts of trained professionals (nor do I or Cobb or Cheydleur). Collins just explains how people have easier access to those who are nearer to them; people who have a genuine concern for their welfare and are available at no cost. Collins also shows that the willingness and genuine concern of friends and family play a huge role in their effectiveness in helping people.

There are many principles of expert knowledge as it relates to the Christian worldview. Many of the principles have underlying presuppositions. It is evident that all ostensible (professed) expert knowledge is not obtained through the scientific (i.e., technical, systematic, exact) process, and is therefore mislabeled as such. There is enough documented information to assist us in discerning which of the principles mentioned should make its way into our Christian worldview and which should not.

How about Homosexuality

One cannot deal with morals and values within Christianity without also answering some questions about homosexuality. Homosexuality has been at the forefront of internal issues for Christians for quite some time. Jeff S. Siker points out in his book, *Homosexuality in the Church: Both Sides of the Debate*, that The Universal Fellowship of Metropolitan Community Churches (whose congregations are predominately comprised of homosexuals: lesbian, gay, bisexual, and transgender) started with a group of twelve in 1968 and celebrated its twenty-fifth year of existence with a conference welcoming members from seventeen nations in 1993. [30] It is obvious then that persons who live what is often referred to as "alternative lifestyles" still seek God and thus Christians must address concerns and debates that arise about homosexuality within the Christian community.

I have found that the debates of which I've been a part have often centered on the question, "Did God create individuals with a homosexual desires or did they somehow develop such a longing at some point on their own?" The sides of the debate often argue if it comes from birth (or naturally) then it had to have come from God, since God created all things in nature. Otherwise, if it was developed, then it's a product of humankind's ingenuity (for lack of a better term) rather than a natural occurrence.

Answering the question, "Is homosexuality natural?" from a purely Biblical view often leads to allegations of being judgmental or in popular terms, 'gay bashing'. This is not the intent here. Christians cannot stand in judgment of anyone, including their own. According to Matthew 7:1, they are not to do so. Matthew 7:1 says, "Do not judge..." It does not give any exceptions or disclaimers. God's intent in this statement is very clear. He retains the responsibility of judgment for Himself, through Jesus Christ. So, to hopefully help minimize the allegations of gay bashing, this section will not flow like a Bible study lesson on homosexuality. It will not discuss the *person*(s) of homosexuality. This section, rather, will be an examination and critique of the *practice* of homosexuality to determine if it comes from natural tendencies or some other source.

This will also not become a debate on whether or not the practice homosexuality is sinful. If one wishes to find that answer they can go straight to the Scriptures and determine that it is sin. One doesn't need to argue or debate that. Consequently, one can also find every other thing that humankind does against God's will, which are also sins, in the Scriptures. If one desires to condemn homosexuals solely on their practice, then they would have to discuss every other sin that is practiced and condemn the people who commit those as well. Of course, that would lead to self-condemnation in the process. Let me complete the sentence in Matthew 7:1 which I began earlier: "Do not judge so that you will not be judged." Romans 3:23 states that *all* have sinned (or practiced acts against God's will). Therefore, again, this section is not a judgment session. It is a critique to assist in debating the question: Is homosexuality natural?

How does a Christian respond to someone who feels that it is natural to be a homosexual? Certainly all Christians are touched by this issue and eventually are forced to form some sort of theological apologetic response (biblical answer) concerning it. In responding to this thing, as with any question that requires a theologically formed response, we must query the Bible to see what our answer should be. In cases where we are trying to explain difficult ideologies we certainly need to maintain a Bible stance, however, we must sometimes go beyond the Bible's verbatim answer and explain the idea in a way that the recipient can better understand it. In other words, the answer must be Biblically sound, but framed in a way a person who is not familiar (or doesn't agree) with the Bible can comprehend it.

The subject of homosexuality is certainly no exception to this rule. Christians must go beyond Bible verses to explain this in a layman manner (a way that is understood by those who are not strongly familiar with Christianity or the Holy Scriptures that govern Christianity). In fact, I would venture to say that we should start without Bible verses in this case, and then move to Bible verses once we've reached agreement in an area where a person has gained awareness (for instance, science, philosophy, culture, etc.). Amos 3:3 states that two people cannot walk together unless they first agree to do so. We cannot walk anyone through the Scriptures to discuss this subject until we get those unfamiliar with Scripture to first understand the same things outside of Scripture. Afterwards, Scriptures can be used to confirm what's already been agreed upon as fact.

This concept of beginning without Scripture to address issues that Christians must address by God's Word may raise the brow of many theologians. Some who are well-versed in (know a lot about) Scripture wish to come straight from the Word of God without hesitation. But examine the concept for a moment. We must empathize (recognize) that a seasoned Christian's level of understanding and faith in the Bible, does not amount to a hill of beans to some non-Christians. Even some other Christians are offended or intimidated by 'deep' discussion of biblical matters. The only chance one might have at engaging some folks in meaningful biblical conversation is by getting them to first understand that the knowledge they have points to a greater knowledge. We can then gradually lead them to that greater knowledge (truth) which can be found in the Bible.

This concept is no different than Paul's concept of becoming "all things to all [people], so that I may by all means save some." (I Corinthians 1:22b - brackets added). Paul was talking about taking what non-Christians or 'new' Christians understood (even though it may have not been biblical) and appealing to their common sense or intellect before taking them to the Scriptures and pointing them to the truth of a matter. In this, Paul presented the gospel in an inviting way rather than an offensive one.

This is the approach he took at *Areopagus* or Mar's Hill (see Acts 17:22-34). Paul addressed the philosophers about their superstitions and the idols they worshipped there. He never criticized; he only made mention that they 'sure had a lot of idols around that hill' (paraphrasing). He keyed in on one of the idols which they had no name for and no concept of. This was an idol (actually a stack of rocks) representing or honoring a god with whom they were unfamiliar. After explaining that he had more information than they on the unknown god they built the idol for, Paul gave them biblical information on this god. Some saw Paul's explanation as interesting, rather than offensive and asked to him to teach them more about the unknown God. By this means, some eventually believed in God.

Their understanding of Bible truth came from a discussion, which examined and analyzed their misguided worship of one of their idol gods. The examination and critique was done in a way that appealed to their common sense (or in this case their intellect), then pointed them to the greater truth. This was a solemn appeal (a serious questioning of), not a slanderous repulsion (poking fun or disrespecting) of their beliefs. We must take the same approach if we are to effectively deal with strong, but wrong, beliefs and practices that a person may have concerning the God of the Bible.

Now... let's begin outside of the Bible with this discussion of homosexuality. We will do it for the same reason that Paul did it. Those guys on Mar's Hill probably would have not given an ear to Paul's message if he had just come straight from Scripture – criticizing and disrespecting their beliefs. That approach would not have been as effective. They either did not understand or did not agree with Scripture. So Paul didn't start with Scripture, even though he knew the answer could be found directly from Scripture. The Bible was clear of who God is, but those philosophers on Mar's Hill were not.

Likewise, the Bible is clear on God's position on homosexuality, even though many people may not be. The willful practice of homosexuality, then, would indicate either disagreement to or misunderstanding of Scripture. If one feels homosexuality is a natural occurrence they are obviously viewing it from a scientific or naturalistic perspective and not from Scripture. So, let's examine and critique homosexuality from a scientific/naturalistic viewpoint first and see if their perspective holds merit (proves logical).

Let's take a look at how the science of psychology views this subject with a quote from the American Psychological Association (APA):

> There are numerous theories about the origins of a person's sexual orientation; most scientists today agree that sexual orientation is most likely the result of a complex interaction of environmental, cognitive and biological factors. In most people, sexual orientation is shaped at an early age.[30]

This statement from the APA gives clear indication that homosexuality is a learned or influenced behavior and not a physiological trait that is present in a person at birth. In simpler terms, homosexuality is something that one must set their mind to do. It is not a natural occurrence that happens at or before birth. Even though psychologists feel it is often shaped at an early age, they do agree that it happens after birth – not at or before birth.

Now that answer is from pure science, but not everyone follows science enough to agree with it; so, a different approach may be warranted for non-scientific types. Since I am the non-scientific type, I may be a good person to offer a different view. I will evaluate this thing against nature, since this is a question of whether or not homosexuality is *natural*. Observance of nature gives us many answers to how things are and must have always been. Several natural sciences base themselves upon this principle. Biology, astronomy, and physics are all disciplines of natural science that take samplings of data from nature and determine facts about the universe that prove constant and therefore established as truths. So, borrowing from their practices, samples from nature can be gathered to determine a truth about homosexuality.

Having grown up in a very rural (country) environment, I have been able to mentally gather a great deal of sample data from nature. I have been around farm animals, house pets and even wild animals my entire life. Never in nature have I seen two animals of the same gender have intercourse or make any gestures that connote (indicate) homosexual relations between the two of them. In all my years of obtaining a higher education, I have not heard or read of such a case in nature from someone else's account, either – neither scholar (teacher) nor novice (student).

With the sample data that that has been obtained over my lifetime (quite a few years), I have formed the strong hypothesis that homosexuality is not natural. Coupling this hypothesis formed on the basis of sampling of natural data with the findings of psychological study, one can deem it a scientific fact (a proven constant or established truth) that homosexuality is not natural.

Providing this information in appeal to someone about the nature of homosexuality, should make it hard for them to debate against the understanding that homosexuality is a learned or chosen lifestyle. Once that is done, we can refer to Scriptures (Romans 1:26-27) to show what the Bible says about homosexuality. We will discuss that a bit later.

We can show how science and nature agrees with God (of course) in that homosexuality is not something God designed in nature. Once it's proven from a biblical, scientific, and natural standpoint that homosexuality is not natural, but rather is a chosen practice, then one can begin to address the reasons why individuals should not choose to practice it.

We can explain the natural health factors surrounding homosexuality. AIDS is a very deadly and still incurable disease that has been propagated (spread) among other ways through homosexual activities. One can explain the social ramifications (effects) of homosexuality. Although it is gaining more and more acceptance within this western culture, it is still a very taboo (the majority doesn't want to get involved in discussions about it) topic. Although more and more proclaimed Christians accept it as okay, the Bible is strongly against it; therefore Bible-based Christianity must oppose the participation in it – still without condemning its participants.

If that is not enough, based on another sampling of data – the observations made in watching homosexuals – we can purport (contend/make the case) that the lifestyle seems to bring more hardship than joy. Those who have chosen this lifestyle appear to always have social difficulties surrounding them. Their lives seem to be filled with anger, bitterness, and just overall dysfunctional. How do I validate these statements? Observation in the workplace with homosexuals for over twenty years reveals they seem to have more sadness than gladness in their lives. Observation of homosexuals in the church setting for much longer produces the same results.

This may seem somewhat judgmental or at least more opinionated than factual but it is not. It is pure observation. Jesus let His disciples know that you can tell a tree by the fruit it bears (see Matt 12:33, Luke 6:44). If you see apple fruit growing on a tree, then you know that it is an apple tree. You don't have to judge or speculate that. You just look at the fruit. So if you observe a person or persons over an extended period of time and they always appear to be unhappy, more likely than not, they are unhappy.

In every case I've observed over time, there was a cloud of apparent unhappiness (or dissatisfaction with life in general) hovering over the individuals. Perhaps this lack of joy in their lives is due to the unjustifiable burden the bulk of society places on homosexuals for choosing that lifestyle. That is a strong possibility. Maybe it is due to inter-relational conflicts that come from the unnatural intertwining of emotions, desires, etc. Maybe it's due to internal spiritual and mental struggles with the choice to go against what spiritually should be. The determination of cause of this dysfunctional tendency is not the intent here. Observation, nonetheless, is convincing that this lifestyle does not bring with it the joy that life should bring to individuals.

Personal observations aside, it is biblically, scientifically, and naturally clear that homosexuality is not a natural inclination. One is not born with this yearning. It is formed by outside influences and has to be contemplated and consented to by the individual who willingly takes part in the activity. One has to get to this point of understanding before they can even begin to address causation (what causes it) and spiritual and moral issues surrounding the subject.

Since we now have this understanding, we *can* ask the question, "What causes it?" Science proves it's not a psychological thing. Nature proves it's not a physiological (natural) thing. Well, if it can't be answered scientifically, and it can't be observed naturally, that leaves only one source. It must be of a spiritual origin. Something in one's spirit or an external spirit must cause them to travel this path which suggests to a person that homosexual behavior is something they would want to partake of. If logic is to play a part in finding the answer, then this is the only logical answer to this thing called homosexuality.

The Bible speaks of good spiritual things and bad spiritual things. This good and bad does not reside in the physiological make up (natural body/ flesh) of a person. If that were the case, medical doctors could cut away what's wrong and solve all the world's physiological problems. Similarly, this spiritual good and bad does not reside in the psychological (mental) make up of a person. If that were the case, Sigmund Freud and his contemporaries would have solved all of the world's 'mental' problems by now through their psychological experiments. Neither the physical nor the psychological approach has resolved any issues with homosexuality, because they cannot address what it is: a spiritual issue.

How do we conclude this debate and begin to resolve the issue? Well, we go to the authority on spiritual things – the Bible. The Bible deals with spiritual things better than any other source. First of all, Romans 1:26-27 (mentioned before) explains clearly that homosexuality goes against nature. Secondly, Galatians 5: 16-17 explains how a person's life is always either under the influence of a good Spirit (the Holy Spirit) or bad spirit (ungodly spirit). The term the Bible uses for bad spirit is "works of the flesh." This Greek word for flesh is *sarx* or "the earthly nature of man apart from divine influence, and therefore prone to sin and opposed to God."

Galatians 5:19-23 gives a long (although not exhaustive [complete]) list of bad spiritual activities and good spiritual activities. The works of the flesh are acts of the person that are influenced from bad spirits that operate outside of the individual and against God. The good spiritual things are called the fruits of the Spirit. They are acts of the person influenced from within by the Holy Spirit (residing inside those who have accepted Christ) and in concert with God.

The first item in the 'works of the flesh' list found in Galatians 5:19-21(New International Version) is sexual immorality or bad sexual practice. What is considered sexual immorality is more evident in a list of bad sexual practices found in I Corinthians 6:9-10 that are associated with a person working in the flesh: fornication – having sex before getting married; adultery – having sex with someone other than your spouse; and homosexuality – having sex with someone of the same gender. For Christians, it's crystal clear that homosexuality is not a lifestyle condoned (acceptable) by God.

From a physical viewpoint, homosexuality is not natural, but still some wonder why and how so many are attracted to it. From a psychological angle, it does not begin at birth, yet still so many are unclear where it has its beginning. However, nothing about homosexuality is a mystery when you view it from a Biblical perspective, which should provide a conclusion to the debate – at least among Christians anyway.

Conclusion

I know this chapter offers terms and discussions that the average young person thinks is either uninteresting or just altogether not really important in the grand scheme of Christianity. There is an important message here for you, though. I didn't collect and write this section to show off my level of learning in the area of common and expert knowledge or philosophies built upon the two. I'm definitely not the 'expert' on any of this. I just took good notes in school.

My purpose for including this information is that the philosophies mentioned in this chapter are highly regarded by many in academia and some who have been well educated in the secular education system. They will be pushed at you as if they are a religion. In fact, to some educators, they are a religion. I had one professor (in a secular college) who got furious when someone made a joke about Socrates. They held Socrates in such high esteem; it was as if the student had ridiculed God Himself.

You must evaluate philosophies carefully before introducing them into your Christian worldview. Carefully consider how some of those philosophies came about and ways some of them contradict with Biblical truth. Consider also how some of their founders fail to follow the scientific process in developing their philosophies. There are very valid reasons for not employing the philosophies mentioned in this chapter as pivotal points in your Christian worldview. (There are good reasons you should not build your Christian worldview around some of these philosophies.) Those we discussed all have assumptions that their originators used acceptable criteria for determining their findings to be true. We have seen, however, that they did not. Rogerianism suggests that humankind is good by nature and has absolutely no need for a Higher Authority (God). We can easily determine otherwise. Freudianism and Skinner's Behaviorism both claim that only certain individuals have the capacity to help others. We know that is not the case. The discussion on homosexuality was included because if one is led to believe that it's a natural occurrence then there's room to infer (conclude) that it's from and of God. We can clearly see that it is not.

The philosophies presented in this chapter are taught in many secular institutions of higher learning, as well as public high schools. In many cases, they clearly contradict with some very core Christian principles. No matter how well they are presented; certain aspects of them should be checked at the door when leaving the classroom. We should not apply them to our Christian worldview. Since much of the philosophy we've discussed in this chapter cannot be applied to the Christian value system, a discussion of what can be applied is our next and final topic: applying the knowledge of God.

7 APPLYING THE KNOWLEDGE OF GOD

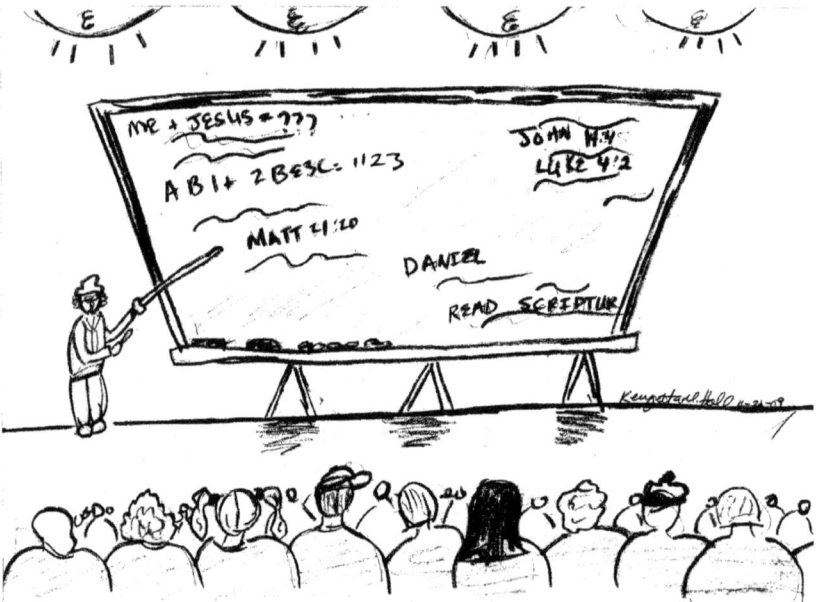

The idea for us as Christians is to discipline ourselves so that the relationship with God does not deteriorate. (Rf. John 14:15)

The Reconciliation/Discipline Dynamic: Review of Reconciliation

Our final discussion involves the application of the knowledge of God. Applying this knowledge means we make it a part of our daily lives. Maintaining our faith means living by our faith. Thus, our faith becomes a part of our habits, our demeanor, and our decision-making, which altogether makes us better Christians. We become more and more like Christ. 1 John 3:2 says that we shall be like Christ. 1 John 3:3 says, "Everyone who has this hope fixed on Him [Christ] purifies himself, just as He [Christ] is pure." (Brackets added.) Remember we found that hope here in the Greek language (elpis) meant "joyful and confident expectation of eternal salvation." So, the Apostle John is saying that everyone who has the hope of eternal salvation purifies him/herself even as Jesus Christ is pure. We begin to live out our faith or apply Christ in our lives or simply put–act like Christians ought to. The only way to act like one should is to discipline oneself to do so.

Before we talk about applying the knowledge of God (in the way of Spiritual discipline), I want to explain the reconciliation/discipline dynamic as it relates to the Christian worldview. This isn't your average Sunday School discussion; but it helps you fully understand the importance of applying this knowledge of God or disciplining yourself Spiritually. It shows why we need discipline ourselves in order to maintain or improve our relationship with God.

The reconciliation/discipline dynamic represents the idea that God disciplines us in order to re-establish the proper relationship between us and Him. Much like the legal system attempts to discipline criminals in its efforts to re-establish their proper relationship with society. The idea for us as Christians (it's the same with the citizen in society), however, is to discipline ourselves, so that our relationship with God doesn't deteriorate (go bad). In the last chapter, we discussed how some folks don't feel that people need any discipline outside of their own. It was also demonstrated that some feel humankind certainly doesn't need a single disciplining Authority (a.k.a. God). We can discipline ourselves to a certain point. Disciplining ourselves is necessary for a good relationship with God; but because of our natural desire to sin (that's been discussed), we sometimes need disciplining beyond what we can or will do for ourselves. Paul explains the difficulty with disciplining ourselves in Romans 7:15. He says, "For what I am doing, I do not understand; for I am not practicing what I would like to do, but I am doing the very thing I hate."

In this next discussion we'll define the levels of the reconciliation/discipline dynamic and its purpose and benefits. We'll discuss how this dynamic is viewed by the modern Christian church. We'll demonstrate that the principles of the dynamic of reconciliation/discipline are clearly defined in Scripture. We'll determine the goal of the reconciliation/discipline dynamic as a component of the Christian worldview. Finally, we'll discuss some ways we can discipline ourselves (Spiritually) and maintain a proper relationship with God.

Prescribed Scripture

The dynamic of reconciliation and discipline has been addressed by a number of authors outside of Scripture. But most of these authors reference Scriptures in explaining the concept. Dr. Jay E. Adams speaks to the subject extensively in The Christian Counselor's Manual. In fact, his method of counseling, which is known as Nouthetic Counseling, is centered on the Biblical principle of the reconciliation/discipline dynamic.

Adams and others who have written on the subject seem to agree that the passage of Scripture which best provides understanding and endorsement (support) of this dynamic is Matthew 18:15-17. Adams includes verses eighteen through twenty in his case. He makes it clear that he feels this passage of Scripture is at the core of the Biblical principle of the reconciliation/discipline dynamic. He writes:

We must consider next an important Biblical principle that provides a basis for hope by spelling out the Biblical dynamic that leads to change. The principle may be stated as the following: interpersonal problems between Christians must be solved. Perhaps this principle is best exemplified by the reconciliation/discipline dynamic. The dynamic is described in Matthew 18:15-20.[1]

Adams details three levels to the reconciliation/discipline dynamic as found in the aforementioned passage.

He offers that the first level involves a one-on-one attempt at reconciling (restoring the relationship of) someone who is in some way out of fellowship with God. By the way, if you're not in the right fellowship with another person; then you're out of fellowship with God as well. 1 John 4:40 tells us, "If someone says, 'I love God' and hates his brother, he is a liar; for the one who does not love his brother whom he has seen, cannot love God whom he has not seen." The first level is addressed best by a single person. If you know a friend or loved one is doing something that will damage their relationship with God, you should address it with them. You should approach them with the intent to help them resolve the issue. It should certainly not be in a condemning (accusing) manner. They will usually heed to the helpful, non-condemning advice or observation of a friend or loved one.

The second level engages two or more persons in the process. Sometimes a person doesn't feel just your opinion is enough to convince them of their wrong. In those cases, usually if more people show them that same wrong, they will heed to the collective advice or observation of a few friends or loved ones.

The third and final level necessitates (requires) the entire church's involvement. In this case, the individual in the wrong generally has no immediate intention of correcting the wrong. But, when they are addressed by their relational group as a whole (i.e., church, family or organization); it usually triggers a desire to not be frowned upon by the group. They almost certainly don't want to be disconnected from the group. Within the final level, although discipline is administered (applied) when the guilty party refuses to repent (correct the wrongful acts), Adams explains that the ultimate goal is even in this tough discipline: reconciliation. He states,

> But even the discipline, n.b. [meaning take notice of this very carefully], has reconciliation in view. Excommunication [being put out of the church] is not an end in itself but, at least temporarily, it settles the matter. Hopefully, this serious act itself at length may bring the offender to repentance [cause them to say they're sorry and change their attitude].2 (Brackets added for clarification.)

So, even if a situation results in discipline by removing someone from the group (in this case the church), the intent is not to get rid of them forever. It is to make them see the seriousness of what they have done and to make them want to restore relationships.

Adams offers his readers some purposes and benefits of the reconciliation/discipline dynamic. As for purposes, he states, "It is done to preserve the honor of God's name, to assure the purity of the church and to reclaim and reconcile the offender."[3] In the way of benefits, he proposes that it provides an effective dynamic for "tying up loose ends"[4] and he reiterates, "The reconciliation/discipline dynamic offers great hope."[5]

Despite the purposes and benefits mentioned by Adams, he maintains that the reconciliation/discipline dynamic "has been almost totally neglected not only by church liberals, but also by the modern conservatives in the Christian church. Church liberals are those who feel the church is too strict. Church conservatives are those who think the church is not strict enough. This lack of discipline is not good, Adams implies, because we need it to maintain a closer relationship with Christ. He states (referencing Matthew 18:20), "The presence of Christ is promised wherever the reconciliation/discipline dynamic is properly set in motion."[6]

According to the group of authors of *Restoring the Fallen*, the Biblical principle of reconciliation and discipline has not been forgotten by the Christian church (as Adams feels). They feel, however, it certainly has *not* been utilized in its entirety. They presume that the church takes one of three approaches to this dynamic. The team of husbands and wives, Earl and Sandy Wilson, Paul and Virginia Frieson, and Larry and Nancy Paulson writes concerning those three approaches:

> The first may be termed "cheap grace"–a quick, non-confronting, short-term approach to the problem: accept the individual's apology and let it go at that... The second approach is the legalistic response, which may result in banishment of the sinner from the church. Some churches call this excommunication... Little thought is given to restoration of the individual to fellowship with God or with the church family... The third and probably most frequent response is to ignore the problem altogether... nothing is made public and the process does not involve accountability or follow-up.[7]

Nouthetic is Nothing New

The authoring group suggests that there is a better (Biblical) way. The authors reference Galatians 6:1-2 in expressing scriptural teaching "discipline and restoration are always tied to a local fellowship."[8] The group then references Matthew 18:15-17 as does Adams when they spell out that "better"[9] way. The better way is the same principle upon which Adams created his Nouthetic Counseling concept, explaining reconciliation/ discipline dynamic of Scripture. The word Nouthetic, by the way, is taken from the Greek word *noutheteō* which means to instruct, correct or encourage.

The authors then offer "nine traits of a restoring church."[10] Out of these traits, items numbered two, three and four exemplify (illustrate) the dynamic of reconciliation and discipline found in Matthew 18:15-17. They are:

- A place where godly judgment is administered
- A place where grace is extended
- A place for discipline.[11]

Dr. Larry Crabb, author of *The Christian Counselor's Manual*, agrees with both Adams and the group of authors of *Restoring the Fallen* on what the Biblical principle of the dynamic of reconciliation/discipline is; referencing Colossians 1:28. Crabb's only caveat (caution) is that he does not feel this "confrontational model," as he terms it, is the only effective Christian disciplining model. I don't think the process has to be confrontational. You don't have to beat someone down to teach them discipline. But there are folks who seem to always approach discipline in a very confrontational way.

From the information presented by the authors, we can clearly recognize the levels, purposes and benefits of the principle of reconciliation/discipline dynamic found in Scripture. However, it may take a more hermeneutical approach to (a more detailed look at) the referenced Scriptures to understand the principle behind the statements of Jesus Christ recorded in Matthew 18:15-17.

Hermeneutical Help

Hermeneutics, according to a lecture by Dr. Ed Glasscock, another professor at Luther Rice University, is "the science and art of interpretation."[12] Science in this sense, again according to Glasscock, involves "objective analysis of the text,"[13] which includes its "vocabulary, grammar, context, content and background."[14] A hermeneutical view of the passage, then, should identify Jesus' principle in this message found in Matthew 18:15-17. Merriam-Webster defines principle as, "a comprehensive and fundamental law, doctrine, or assumption."[15] In that respect, we can define principle as *Jesus' doctrine (His teaching, instruction) or fundamental law (His expected course of actions) for His followers.*

The passage of Scriptures in Matthew 18:15-17 (KJV) reads as follows:

Moreover if thy brother shall trespass against thee, go and tell him his fault between thee and him alone: if he shall hear thee, thou hast gained thy brother. But if he will not hear thee, then take with thee one or two more, that in the mouth of two or three witnesses every word may be established. And if he shall neglect to hear them, tell it unto the church: but if he neglects to hear the church, let him be unto thee as an heathen man and a publican.[16]

In keeping with proper hermeneutical practice, you should read through the background to better understand the content of the immediate passage of Scripture. The background in this case is the entire eighteenth chapter of Matthew.

Of course, we should then obtain definitions for key words in the passage and ensure that we do not misinterpret the meaning. By finding the original Greek meaning of the key words, we can put together an understandable (modern English) statement of what the text says. Having the correct interpretation, we can determine the message and central idea of the text.

The message is that if one person is wronged by another or determines another is doing wrong, we should go to the person and plead with them to correct the wrong. If the person corrects the wrong, then we have caused that person to be spared discipline for the wrongdoing and to be restored to right relationships. If the person refuses to hear, then we are to take one or more witnesses and go back to the person and make another attempt at getting that person to correct his or her action(s). If then, the person continues refusal of correction ('refuses to repent' fits nicely here), the church as a body should attempt to get the person to correct his or her action(s). If at that point, the person yet refuses, then discipline is called upon, which involves alienation (removing the person from the church). A shorter version of the central idea of the text is when someone strays away from the will of God the church is to make every attempt at reconciling them back to God. If that person refuses reconciliation, then we must discipline them. Thus, what our referenced authors have suggested is confirmed in Scripture.

There is one matter of business we still need to address concerning this, and then we can move on. (Did I hear a sigh of relief?) Adams stated that the purpose of discipline is the "honor of God's name, to assure the purity of the church and to reclaim and reconcile the offender." We still need to address reconciling the offender. This is the ultimate goal in the disciplining process. Adams does not offer the following two Scriptures as Biblical backing of this statement, but I think they will help make his point.

The first passage is found in 2 Peter 3:9. It states, "The Lord is not slow about His promise, as some count slowness, but is patient toward you, *not wishing for any to perish but for all to come to repentance.*" The second passage of Scripture is found in Ezekiel 33:11. It states, "Say to them, 'As I live!' declares the Lord GOD, *'I take no pleasure in the death of the wicked, but rather that the wicked turn from his way and live.* Turn back, turn back from your evil ways! Why then will you die, O house of Israel?" (Italics added, in both cases, for emphasis.)

The passages of Scripture in 2 Peter and Ezekiel agree with Adams' statement or I should say, Adams' statement agrees with them: God's ultimate goal in this discipline portion of the reconciliation/discipline dynamic is "to reclaim and reconcile the offender." He will discipline us to motivate us into renewing a proper relationship with Him. God, however, prefers that the offender makes the first effort in restoring or maintaining the right relationship with Him.

If you think about it, parents (good parents) attempt to offer the same grace as God does. Haven't you ever had a parent offer you the opportunity to correct your wrongful action, before issuing you punishment? Even if it's with the threatening phrase, "Don't let me have to tell you again! Don't make me come over there! Don't make me stop this car!" It may be offered as a threat, but it is still another chance; an offer of grace. Well, if your parents (or teachers or coaches, etc.) being imperfect can offer this type of grace, think how much more God can (being a perfect God).

We can conclude that the dynamic of reconciliation/discipline has three levels and involves everybody in the church. But, it has only one goal: re-establishing the proper relationship between God and humankind. But again, the best thing for the Christian is to discipline self, so that the relationship does not deteriorate. When folks want their bodies to be healthy for living a good, long life, they discipline themselves to eat right (most of the time) and exercise regularly. This physical discipline improves the health for longevity of life. The body doesn't deteriorate so easily. That's the reason for Spiritual discipline (disciplining ourselves in a Spiritual manner). It improves the health of our relationship with God and others. So, our final discussion will cover the topic of Spiritual Discipline.

Spiritual Discipline

By the way, when the word Spiritual is capitalized, it is to distinguish (help you tell the difference) between a Godly Spirit and an ungodly spirit. Many authors write concerning spirituality and spiritual things, but we must be careful of what spirits those authors are writing about. They are not all Godly.

The passage of Scripture found in 1 John 4:1 warns us Christians to be careful of which spiritual influence we follow. It reads, "Beloved, do not believe every spirit, but test the spirits to see whether they are from God…" Many religions encourage spiritual discipline, but those referred to in this book refer to disciplining ourselves in Godliness. The purpose for disciplining ourselves in Godliness is so we might be more and more what God desires of us.

Just to recap and build on what was discussed earlier in Chapter 3, God created humankind with the intent of humankind glorifying Him. This is spelled out in Isaiah 43:7. The way humankind glorifies God is by reflecting God's glory back to Him. We could do this because we were created in His image as stated in Genesis 1:26-27. After Adam's sin, humankind could no longer reflect God's glory or glorify God as He intended. Humankind had fallen short of the glory it possessed at creation. Romans 3:23 makes us aware of this. Dr. Jim Kinnebrew (yet another professor at Luther Rice University—they're everywhere) puts it this way: "[Being short of God's glory is] As the moon is when behind the earth cannot receive the sun's light or reflect that light."[18] (Brackets added.) Dr. David Platt puts it: "[Being short of God's glory is] as a mirror that is distorted or tarnished cannot reflect a perfect image." (Brackets added.)

God restored this glory to humankind in His Son, Jesus Christ as declared in John 1:1-2, 14. Verses 1 and 2 show that Jesus is God and verse 14 shows He is indeed man and "...we beheld his glory, the glory as of the only begotten of the Father, full of grace and truth." Unlike the fallen man, He is the perfect image of God as Hebrews 1:3 gives account.

Jesus made provisions for humankind to have the glory His Father gave to Him. We see this in John 17:22 when He states that he has given those who are in Him (i.e., Christians) the glory which His Father gave Him. Colossians 1:7 states also that humankind has this hope of glory through Christ in them. We aren't to just sit on this glory and wait for it to be manifested in the day of Christ; however, we are to cultivate (grow, nurture) it into a form of Godliness by disciplining ourselves Spiritually as seen in 1 Timothy 4:7.

Donald S. Whitney, author of *Spiritual Disciplines for the Christian Life* makes the point that God uses three different "catalysts" (boosters) in triggering our growth into His glory or as Whitney puts it, the "image of Christ." Whitney feels the three means by which God stimulates growth toward this image are circumstances in our lives, people whom we encounter, and our Spiritual disciplines. I believe we respond to circumstances in our lives and deal with people we encounter the way God intended *if* we have disciplined ourselves Spiritually. For this reason, our conversation will conclude with a presentation of ways we might achieve Spiritual discipline.

It is of utmost importance, first, that I remind you of the danger of believing that to grow into the glory of God and the image of Christ means we somehow begin to become deity (a god). That is not the case. The idea of growing into the grace of God and image of Christ simply means we begin to act and feel like we belong to God. That is the image we were created with.

There is a passage of Scripture which has been taken out of context (used incorrectly), to make folks believe that humankind will become gods somehow. One well-established religion identifying itself with Christianity actually teaches this. The passage I'm referring to is 2 Peter 1:4 and it reads, "Whereby are given unto us exceeding great and precious promises: that by these *ye might be partakers of the divine nature*, having escaped the corruption that is in the world through lust." (Emphasis added.)

Those who take this passage out of context believe that becoming a partaker of divine nature makes us a deity. The Greek word for nature here (*phusis*), however, is "a mode of feeling and acting which by long habit has become nature." So, the things that are changing about Christians are our feelings, actions and/or habits, so that we might do and think in the same manner as God. It is saying we will continue to increasingly act in a Godly manner. You know, portray the correct image of God like we were created to do. We don't become God as some religions suggest. Understanding of the Greek context and reading the text surrounding this passage of Scripture reveals that Peter is explaining a process of growth of a Christian's character and not a metamorphosis of their body or spirit into a deity.

Peter points out key things in this passage that provide understanding of how the original text defines 'nature'. The most simple, yet most convincing thing is the small word, "the" in verse 4. Peter does not say "[*His*] divine nature, but rather "*the* divine nature." We should understand "the divine nature" as character surrounding God; whereas, "[His] divine nature" would have meant His actual fullness of deity. Remember, we discussed how John 1:14 proves the deity of Jesus Christ. Well, John uses "*His* glory" in that text, referring to the <u>fullness of deity</u>. Here, however, Peter uses "*the* glory" signifying <u>the character surrounding God</u>. Jamieson, Fausset, and Brown offer rationale for defining divine this way in their commentary on this portion of verse 4: "*the divine nature* -- not God's essence, but His holiness."[17] (Emphasis added.)

The Holy Spirit guides Peter into taking painstaking (particular) care in presenting this "Growth in Christian Virtue" as a work of God, through the Holy Spirit in the person. It is not something the individual does by themselves. By the way, "Growth in Christian Virtue" is the title the NASB gives this group of Scriptures found in 2 Peter 1:1-15. I don't want to take credit for that clever caption.

The individual is not growing into a divine person. He or she is, rather, submitting more and more to the divine person of God—the Holy Spirit—within them. Matthew Henry alludes to this fact in his commentary on this passage of Scriptures. He writes, "Those in whom the Spirit works the divine nature are freed from the bondage of corruption."[18]

Finally, Peter vividly presents an order of growth in the individual's willingness to submit to holiness or Godliness:

- This growth begins with our increasing knowledge of God. Peter says, "Grace and peace be multiplied to you in the *knowledge of God and of Jesus our Lord*; seeing that His divine power has granted to us everything pertaining to life and godliness, through the true knowledge of Him who called us by His own glory and excellence (vv 2,3)." (Emphasis added.) This is the reason I place Bible intake first in importance among the Spiritual disciplines.

- That Spiritual growth blossoms into a lifestyle or set of characteristics that emit (release) the characteristics of God sown within us by the Holy Spirit. Peter writes, "For by these He has granted to us His precious and magnificent promises, so that by them you may become partakers of the divine nature, having escaped the corruption that is in the world by lust (v 4)."

- After blossoming, it bears good fruit (produces positive attitude and actions) through our demeanor (character), causing us to conform to the Spirit of Christ in us. In Peter's words, "Now for this very reason also, applying all diligence, in your faith supply moral excellence, and in your moral excellence, knowledge, and in your knowledge, self-control, and in your self-control, perseverance, and in your perseverance, godliness, and in your godliness, brotherly kindness, and in your brotherly kindness, love [The basic moral element of Christianity, remember?]. For if these qualities are yours and are increasing, they render you neither useless nor unfruitful in the true knowledge of our Lord Jesus Christ (vv 5-8)." (Brackets added.)

I believe this passage of Scripture could easily be the basis for St. Richard of Chichester's prayer, "…know thee more clearly, love thee more dearly, follow thee more nearly…" I know you're thinking "Richard Who?" He was a professor at Oxford University in England back in the 1200's (yeah, before your grandparents). He later became a bishop and held a very high position in church leadership (not much lower than the king). He was well respected and known for his efforts in 'cleaning up' moral issues in the church (He corrected a lot of bad behavior by church leaders.)

• Notice how the passage starts with our "knowledge of God and of Jesus our Lord (v 2, 3)" causing us to *know Him more clearly.*

• Peter shows, then, how we *love God more dearly* as we "apply all diligence in our faith" (v 5).

• Finally, Peter shows how we allow the disciplines to bloom as we begin to increasingly conform to them (*or follow God more nearly*) throughout verses 5-8.

This passage is also the basis for a lecture handout provided by Dr. Kinnebrew in one of his Spiritual Formations classes entitled, "I am a Success." Dr. Kinnebrew's pamphlet gives eight stages to this growth process identified by Peter. They are:

• I have a realization (how ever faint) that Jesus loves me VERY MUCH!

• Because of His wondrous love for me, I love Him.

• Because of my love for Him, I seek to obey Him (and when I stumble, I repent and receive His Grace).

- When I live in obedience to Him and keep short accounts [repent of wrongs as soon as they happen and don't repeat them] with Him through confession and repentance, I enjoy His loving presence.

- When I am walking in conscious fellowship with Him, I naturally "bear fruit" like Love, Joy, Peace, etc.

- When my life is characterized by these God-like qualities, God is glorified in my body. His wonderfulness is seen on earth.

- When God's Glory is reflected on earth through me, I have fulfilled the purpose for which He created me as His Image-bearer.

- If I am fulfilling the purpose for which God created me, I am a SUCCESS![19] (Brackets Added.)

There have been several books written on the subject of Spiritual discipline. The different authors of those books offer numerous ways of expressing how Christians should discipline themselves in a Spiritual manner. After reviewing various lists from different authors, I have found that the following practices of Spiritual disciplines are common among the authors: Biblical intake, prayer, worship, and witness. We discussed witnessing under the heading of Evangelism in Chapter 3, "Sharing the Knowledge of God." Let's now discuss Biblical intake, prayer, and worship. There are other disciplines mentioned by some of the authors (e.g., meditation, silence and solitude, service, and stewardship), but the ones discussed here, I feel, are key for getting a good grounding in the Christian faith. They really need to be in place before the others can be engaged properly.

Biblical Base

The key to disciplining yourself Spiritually is to make sure your worldview has a good Biblical base. So the first of the disciplines to be discussed is Biblical intake. Bible intake is primarily Bible study. We must study the Bible if we are to know God and we must know God if we are to glorify God.

During Seminary, whenever I encountered a professor I had not studied under before, I would find a moment to ask them which version of the Bible they preferred to study from. I found that the New American Standard Bible (NASB) was the most popular. I also got the New International Version (NIV) and King James Version (KJV) as favorable choices. So, I recommend one of these three to you for your Bible study time. Better yet, I suggest you use the KJV and one of the others along with it. The KJV seems the most widely recognized in Christian churches, so when you talk Scripture with folks, you want to be familiar with the KJV.

I also recommend that you spend some time at the following two web sites: *www.biblegateway.com* and *www.biblestudytools.com*. The web sites offer excellent tools for studying the Bible. The first site gives you a means for searching Scriptures based on key words, verses, or topics in many different versions and languages of the Bible. The second offers lexicons (translators/dictionaries) for finding out the Greek and Hebrew meaning of words in the Bible. It also offers commentaries, encyclopedias, and various tools for studying the Bible.

The apostle Paul knew the importance of Bible study. While he was preparing young Timothy to be pastor of a church in Ephesus, he gave him absolute musts which he had to follow in being a good communicator of his knowledge of God in Christ. 2 Timothy 2:15 may have been the most important lesson Paul shared with Timothy regarding Bible intake. It may be the most important lesson that God's Word shares with any of us on the subject. Again, it states, "Study to shew thyself approved unto God, a workman that needeth not to be ashamed, rightly dividing the word of truth (KJV)."

Two men, Art Rorheim and Lance Latham, thought this message was so important that they established a worldwide ministry for young people based on this one passage in the Bible. You may have heard of it. This youth ministry is called AWANA (an acronym for Approved Workmen Are Not Ashamed) and is based out of the suburbs of Chicago, Illinois. According to their website, www.awana.org, more than 22,000 churches and Christian organizations (as of 2011) in all fifty of the United States as well as other countries use its program. How can such a small verse of scripture have such a positively powerful impact? It is because this verse is an absolute, essential element in the Christian faith. Let's take a look at the breakdown of the message in 2 Timothy 2:15 to see just how essential it is:

Study–the act of obtaining knowledge; seeking knowledge [to get familiar with].

Why study God's Word? We can't know Him unless we have been exposed to the medium (the channel of communication) by which He presents Himself to us. That channel of communication is His Word–The Holy Bible. Studying God's Word means more than just casually reading about Him. It means making a concentrated effort in getting to know Him. It means asking questions and finding resources to help you understand the things you don't understand when you casually read it.

If we are going to make it at anything in life, we have to study. Before we learned to walk, we had to study folks around us to see how they managed to get around so easily. Before we learned how to talk, we had to study how they formed words that could be understood by others. We could move our legs and move our lips, but the results just weren't the same as those we studied around us. Not until we watched and listened to (studied) for a while did we start to get better with managing our own.

All through grade school and high school we had to study to make the grade. In most cases we didn't have a choice because teachers and parents were pushing us to do so. If and when we decide to go to college, we will have to study; in most cases harder. And this time, we won't have teachers and parents disciplining us to do so.

We'll have to discipline ourselves. If we decide to venture into the world and pursue a career, the same thing applies.

It doesn't matter how we decide to make our mark (or our living); we will have to study–no matter what we decide to be. Doctors, lawyers, business people all have to constantly study for learning procedures, defending clients, and presenting material to co-workers and customers. Sales clerks have to learn products and prices. Custodians have to learn schedules and new ways of cutting down the number of tasks they have. Even a bum on the street has to constantly learn better ways of how and who to approach for a handout.

If studying is so important for our everyday walk in life, surely it must be extremely important for our Christian walk. Psalm 1:2 says, "But his [a person with a good relationship with God] delight is in the *law of the Lord* [Hebrew–*towrah*: body of legal directions (as in written commandments–the Bible)] and on his law he *meditates* [Hebrew–*siyach*: studies] day and night." (Brackets added for clarity.) A Christian should always be studying the Word of God. Each decision we make in life should depend on what the Scriptures say. That doesn't mean we have to keep a Bible tucked under our arm everywhere we go and open it each time we have to make a decision. But each decision we make should be a Godly one; and if we are going to know which decisions will be Godly ones, we must know God. We know God through studying His word.

To shew thyself <u>approved</u>–of favorable opinion; accepted as satisfactory.

As we mature in Christ, we will get the urge or courage or desire and the opportunity to talk to someone about God. Some of those people will be Christians; some will be non-Christians. It's obvious that we must know what we are talking about if we are to persuade others to consider Christianity. And we will certainly have to know what we are talking about if we are going to challenge other beliefs some folks will bring our way. If we are going to challenge them, we had better make sure that what we say is approved of God (i.e., is Bible-based). Believe it or not, there are a lot of *non*-Christians who know a lot about the Bible. If we are going to try and convince them of something pertaining to God's word, we will need to be well prepared.

Showing we are approved means that we Christians must make a good representation of Jesus Christ when we are spreading His word. That goes far beyond quoting Scriptures. We must know it enough to live it as well. Christ must approve of our actions, our interactions with others, and our general attitude. Others will be able to see that approval of Christ in us as they see our lives lining up with the Word of God. They will see it in our lifestyle; and they will see it in the way God blesses us. (cf. Psalm 1, Proverbs 11:27, and Hebrews 11:6.)

unto God

We shouldn't study God's Word just for the sake of out-talking someone else about it, or to prove to people how intelligent we are with it. Our sole purpose in studying God's Word is to gain understanding of Him–period. We should have no other motives. We should have no personal agendas. We should only have a strong desire to know God better. Again, if we know Him better, we will love Him better; and then we will serve Him better. Two of the three verses referenced above use the word diligently (Proverbs 11:27 and Hebrews 11:6). Diligent means with earnest and energetic effort. We want to give our most earnest effort in our study so that God approves of how we live by and share His Word.

A workman

We are workers for Jesus Christ. In 2 Corinthians 6:1 Paul refers to us as such: "We then as workers together with him [Jesus]…" (Brackets added.) We can look at the end of chapter 5– specifically the last two verses (20 and 21)–and see that Paul's "him" means Jesus. That means we know we have a job to do, and we should come to work prepared to do that job. That preparation comes from lots of study. If a builder does a good job of building a house, it's because they studied the blueprints thoroughly. If we have a good relationship with God and with people, it's because we have studied God's blueprints (His Word) thoroughly.

that need not be ashamed

If we have studied as we should and know God as we should and understand what Jesus requires of us, then we won't be ashamed to share what we know with others. We can speak with confidence (not arrogance) when discussing Biblical truth. We will have an answer to give those who ask why we believe what we believe.

rightly dividing the Word of truth.

This is most crucial. 'Rightly divide' (as stated in chapter 3) is a compound word in Greek: *orthotomeo*, which means cut straight. The Bible writers used terminology and situations the people were very familiar with at the time. Carpentry was a well-established trade, and the terms associated with this trade were well-known.

This compound word had a lot of significance in the carpentry field. If a carpenter did not make his cuts straight, then he would be making a mess of whatever he was building. Things would not line up as they should. The carpenter had to make the right cuts, especially when building the foundation of whatever he was making.

Paul was providing Timothy with his foundational education for ministry. He was teaching Timothy that he had to cut the Word straight (teach it correctly), or whatever ministry he would begin to build at Ephesus would wind up being a mess. He could wind up not giving the people an accurate account of the Word of God. They would then have the wrong understanding of God, and their relationship with God would not be what God intended.

Christians need to teach, evangelize, and share the Word of God correctly. Not only that, we need to live it correctly. If not, we can mislead and confuse others—especially those who are interested in or new to Christianity. We can cause those folks to question, have the wrong perception of or even not believe in God. That would be a terrible offense. Remember what Matthew 18:6 says? It states, "…whoever causes one of these little ones who believe in Me to stumble, it would be better for him to have a heavy millstone hung around his neck, and to be drowned in the depth of the sea." It is a serious matter to share the Word of God incorrectly. We can't get the Word out correctly until we have disciplined ourselves to a point where we take it in correctly. Bible intake is a very important Spiritual discipline.

Proactive Prayer

I have a friend I once worked with who is a tennis player. I never saw her play, but she must be pretty good, because she was telling me about a tournament where she had advanced to the second round before having to yield to a rain delay. The games would resume later, so she sent me a phone text, which said, "Match just got rained out, so I need a rollover prayer." I guess that works like rollover minutes from AT&T. You just save them for when you need them. I sort of took it as nonchalant, you know, how it is when we kind of casually ask someone to pray for us. So, I thought nothing else of it. The next day I sent her a text back and asked how the game went. She responded that she won the first set, but lost the second two (5-7 and 6-7, which is very close), thus losing the game. I responded back to her, "Awe, man! Either you gotta work on your game or we gotta work on our prayer life." It was a little humor to ease the pain of losing, but we all really do need to spend time working on our prayer life.

Most Christians, if you ask them "What is prayer," will respond that it is communicating with God. Even Merriam-Webster agrees that it is "an address (as a petition) to God or a god in word or thought." Of course, Merriam-Webster takes a much more neutral stance here than we do as to Whom we pray to. Prayer by definition is communication with God. Each of us really needs to have a good communication line to God. We should all have the same fervor (passion) each time we communicate with Him.

We all should have the same passion, but the way we communicate with God can be as different as the way we communicate with a parent. Some youth are very comfortable talking with their parents on any given subject. Some are hesitant to talk about certain issues. However, most youth will communicate well with their parents in the confinement of their homes, cars or other private areas better than they will in the public environment. Communication with God is no different. The process flows better when we are in a secluded (private) area where we can confide in Him.

Kenneth Boa, author of *Conformed to His Image*, places a certain emphasis on praying in solitude (alone). In fact, he begins his section on prayer with the statement: "The discipline of prayer is usually associated with a personal dialogue (colloquy [discussion]) with God..."[20] (Brackets added.) Prayer in solitude is essential in one's relationship with God.

There are times, however, when it's appropriate to pray among others. In the Christian church, it is very common for someone to pray out loud during the service—sometimes on more than one occasion. This is called corporate prayer, and its purpose is to edify (improve) the church (or whatever other group is gathered) as a whole. As church/group members pray for one another, it encourages them to know someone else is concerned for their welfare. It also strengthens their faith when they see the results as God answers those prayers. Whitney makes a very good point about corporate prayer. He says,

> Praying regularly with others can be one of the most enriching adventures of your Christian life. Most of the great movements of God can be traced to a small group of people He called together to begin in prayer.[22]

Those authors and several others have many good things to say about different types of prayer rendered to God, but the best place to learn about how you (personally) should pray is the Bible. Matthew 6:5-15 records Jesus' teachings on prayer, and they are very clear as to how one ought to partake in this Spiritual discipline. Here is a copy of those verses (from the King James Version of the Bible) along with my comments in brackets for clarification. The Bible verses are underlined to help you keep my words and Scriptures separate:

[5]And when thou prayest, thou shalt not be as the hypocrites are [the Greek word for hypocrite is *hupocrite* and it means pretenders; stage actors—remember this. It's important]: for they love to pray standing in the synagogues and in the corners of the streets, that they may be seen of men. Verily I say unto you, They have their reward. [It seems this practice of praying out loud at church or in public has been going on for quite some time. The group or public setting is not the issue here (as we just saw in the case of corporate prayer). The problem is when the person praying is not sincere with their prayer. It's when they are just putting on a front (stage acting—remember that phrase?). Although it may be popular, it is not proper. Again, this does not speak against corporate prayer. It speaks against those who wish to show off their oratory (speaking) ability rather than genuinely give God thanks or seek His guidance/help for others. So, if you are asked to conduct corporate prayer (pray in a group setting), be sure your prayer is sincere. Your most personal prayer, however, is one done in solitude.]

[6]But thou, when thou prayest, enter into thy closet, and when thou hast shut thy door, pray to thy Father which is in secret [This gives reinforcement to the previous discussion on prayer in solitude.]; and thy Father which seeth in secret shall reward thee openly [The Greek word for openly is *phaneros* and it means plainly recognized or known. Being openly blessed by God allows everyone to recognize how blessed you are without you having to publicize it (show it off).]

[7]But when ye pray, use not vain repetitions [The Greek word for vain repetitions is *battalogeo* and it means repeating the same things over and over; to babble.], as the heathen do: for they think that they shall be heard for their much speaking. [This is another practice that seems to be common in churches today. Some folks repeat themselves so much you almost know what they are going to say before they begin to pray. Some of them are asked to pray about a certain thing and their prayer lasts forever. Okay, not quite *that* long (forever is a long time), but they seem to be too long. Whitney states, "These kind of prayers are rarely from the heart. God is not the audience being addressed. In reality these prayers are offered to impress the other people who are listening."[23] It may seem at first glance that Whitney and I are being judgmental, but if you back up to verse 5 to the portion I asked you to remember and look at this verse, Jesus says basically the same thing. Hmmm.]

[8]Be not ye therefore like unto them: for your Father knoweth what things ye have need of, before ye ask him. [Jesus gives clear instruction for us to not follow this pattern.]

[9]After this manner therefore pray ye: Our Father which art in heaven, Hallowed be thy name. [The first order of business in prayer is to reverence (respect) God as a holy God.]

[10]Thy kingdom come [We pray for Jesus' return to set up God's new kingdom, and for His Spirit to come now and take up residence in our hearts], Thy will be done in earth, as it is in

heaven [We pray that people would conduct themselves as God would have them to].

[11]Give us this day our daily bread. [We seek God as the source of our needs everyday.]

[12]And forgive us our debts, as we forgive our debtors. [We ask for forgiveness of our wrongdoings and make a statement to forgive others of their wrongdoings towards us.]

[13]And lead us not into temptation, but deliver us from evil [We pray that we are not tempted to do wrong and that no harm comes to us.]: For thine is the kingdom, and the power, and the glory, for ever. Amen [We end the prayer with the same reverence for God as we began with.]

[14]For if ye forgive men their trespasses, your heavenly Father will also forgive you:

[15]But if ye forgive not men their trespasses, neither will your Father forgive your trespasses. [After the prayer, Jesus reiterates (states again) the importance of forgiveness. Forgiveness is absolutely critical in our relationships with both God and other people.]

Look at what Micah 7:18-19 has to say about God's forgiveness:

Who is a God like unto thee, that pardoneth iniquity [forgives sin], and passeth by the transgression of the remnant of his heritage?

He retaineth not his *anger* forever, because he delighteth in mercy. He will turn again, he will have compassion upon us; he will subdue our iniquities; and thou wilt cast all their sins into the depths of the sea. (KJV–Brackets added.)

Remember, the purpose of disciplining ourselves Spiritually is so that we become more like what God wants us to be. He wants us to be like Him. The ability to forgive is a good 'God-likeness' indicator. Forgiving is simply allowing what someone has done wrong to you to pass. Forgiveness is letting it go. Although we can't totally forget (as God can), we can let go.

Communication with God is an important part of our relationship with Him–just as communication is in any relationship. It is so important that Jesus took time to explain in detail (as just demonstrated) how we should and should not go about praying to God. Prayer is important to us both individually and as a community of believers. The Apostle James makes this clear. The passage of Scripture in James 5:15 and 16 reads, "And the prayer offered in faith will restore the one who is sick, and the Lord will raise him up, and if he has committed sins, they will be forgiven him. Therefore, confess your sins to one another, and pray for one another so that you may be healed. The effective prayer of a righteous man can accomplish much."

Unwavering Worship

Our final look at the *Merriam-Webster's Desk Dictionary* offers the definition of worship as "reverence offered a divine being or supernatural power; also: an act of expressing such reverence." To reverence means to show respect. To worship follows the example Jesus gave at the beginning and ending of His model prayer as He reverenced God. Worship of God has been an apparent major part of humankind's relationship with God for a long time. As early as in the fourth chapter of Genesis, we can see evidence of humankind worshipping God as Cain and Abel made offerings unto Him, reverencing Him as the divine Being. It was a simple and perhaps crude form of worship, but it was nonetheless a form of reverence; therefore, it was worship.

Worship took on a more formal setting as time went by and rules and traditions were set into place for God's people as to how they would conduct 'worship service'. At one point, the tabernacle (a temporary dwelling place of God) was used in worship and went with the Israelites wherever they went. Sometime later, a temple was built, which would be the only place to worship and present offerings. They also would praise God, pray to God and impart the word of God to people who attended worship service. After a dispute within the Israelite community, a second temple was built which created some debate among them as to which place was the right place to go and worship God. Finally, Jesus declared that there was no one specific place to worship God, only that people should worship Him in Spirit and in truth (cf. John 4:20-24). This declaration ushered (guided) us into the era of church worship.

Some very distinct elements of temple worship services survived and became a part of the church worship service. According to Dr. Kinnebrew, they are "praise, prayer, and preaching [imparting of the Word of God]." (Brackets added.) As you study Biblical history, you will see that those were elements in Old Testament temple worship. They are obvious elements seen in Christian churches today. They are a vital part of the Spiritual growth process. We should, therefore, discipline ourselves into being not only present regularly at church worship service, but also actively involved in the worship service. This is how we become better Christians and help others to become better Christians. This is the message found in Hebrews 10:22-25. Looks familiar, doesn't it? We've discussed it a couple of times, but it still is worth mentioning again. In fact it's a good Scripture for us to close this discussion on Spiritual discipline:

> ²²Let us draw near with a sincere heart in full assurance of faith, having our hearts sprinkled clean from an evil conscience and our bodies washed with pure water. ²³Let us hold fast the confession of our hope without wavering, for He who promised is faithful; ²⁴and let us consider how to stimulate one another to love and good deeds, ²⁵*not forsaking our own assembling together*, as is the habit of some, but encouraging one another; and all the more as you see the day drawing near. (Emphasis added.)

Conclusion

We must discipline ourselves in what we know about God and Jesus Christ if we are to grow closer to God and if we are to be effective in showing Christ to others. Through Biblical intake, prayer, worship and sharing of the Gospel, we grow stronger in what we know about God. Our theology improves. As we grow stronger in what we know about God, we grow stronger in how we relate to God. It has a very positive effect on our Christian belief system—our moral values, actions, reactions, and overall demeanor (attitude). It not only makes us better, but it also makes us very useful in the spreading of the Christian faith. 2 Peter 2:2-8 lets us know this. We discussed it briefly before. It states:

> [2]Grace and peace be multiplied to you in the knowledge of God and of Jesus our Lord; [3]seeing that His divine power has granted to us everything pertaining to life and godliness, through the true knowledge of Him who called us by His own glory and excellence. [4]For by these He has granted to us His precious and magnificent promises, so that by them you may become partakers of the divine nature, having escaped the corruption that is in the world by lust. [5]Now for this very reason also, applying all diligence, in your faith supply moral excellence, and in your moral excellence, knowledge, [6]and in your knowledge, self-control, and in your self-control, perseverance, and in your perseverance, godliness, [7]and in your godliness, brotherly kindness, and in your brotherly kindness, love. [8]For if these qualities are yours and are increasing, they render you

neither useless nor unfruitful in the true knowledge of our Lord Jesus Christ.

POSTSCRIPT

This relationship between you and God is one of constant growth. It begins as you obtain knowledge of God. It grows as you share that knowledge of God with others. It solidifies as you prove the knowledge of God. It strengthens as you reprove and expose the knowledge of man which attempts to discredit or nullify the knowledge of God. It manifests itself in you (becomes noticeable by others) as you apply the knowledge of God.

Prepared with the knowledge of God, every young Christian can and will continue in a very meaningful and fulfilling relationship with Him through Jesus Christ. This knowledge of God, the foundational understanding of God's Word (which is required to know who He is; and to accept the salvation He offers through His Son, Jesus Christ). That foundation cannot be taken away. It places the potential there for your continuous growth toward a perfect relationship with God through Jesus Christ. It only needs to be coupled with your aspiration.

Hopefully, some of the information presented here, even if it is only two or three statements on two or three pages, has in some way encouraged you to continue your walk of faith in God through Jesus Christ. I also hope something here has prepared you to share and/or defend your faith in whatever setting you find yourself in the next stage of life. College, military or the workforce can be a very trying experience on your Christian faith. It can also be an excellent opportunity for you to display and share your faith.

I pray that you will exceed in every test and take advantage of every opportunity. Every chance you get to witness about the good news of Jesus, I hope you take it. Whether it's increasing somebody's knowledge of God or correcting someone's misunderstanding of Him, I pray you will make the most of every opportunity. Through your efforts, some will be saved; others will be encouraged.

As I close, I would like your prayers for us old folks, too, that we will do the same. Pray that we won't be slack in our responsibilities in spreading and defending the good news. Pray that we will take every opportunity and make every effort to further the Gospel. Pray that we will continue to do our best to prepare you to succeed in your efforts to be whatever you are called to be and encourage you as you do succeed. We have no doubts that you will.

Finally, as the Apostle Paul records in Ephesians 6:19-20:

"and pray on my behalf, that utterance may be given to me in the opening of my mouth, to make known with boldness the mystery of the gospel, for which I am an ambassador in chains; that in proclaiming it I may speak boldly, as I ought to speak."

END NOTES

Introduction

[1]Tom Bisset, *Why Christian Kids Leave the Faith*, (Grand Rapids, MI: Discovery House Publishers, 1992), 22.

[2]Ibid., 22.

Chapter One

[1]*The New American Standard Bible.* (Grand Rapids, MI: Zondervan Corporation, 1999).

[2]Georges Abbott-Smith, *A Manual Greek Lexicon of the New Testament.* (Edinburg: T and T. Clark, 1948).

[3]Francis Brown, C. Briggs, S.R. Driver *The Brown-Driver-Briggs Hebrew and English Lexicon* (Peabody, MA: Hendricks Publishers, 1966)

Chapter Three

[1]Paul E. Little, *How to Give Away Your Faith* (Downers Grove, Ill: InterVarsity Press, 1966), 105.

[2]Dean Finley, *Handbook for Youth Evangelism* (Nashville: Broadman Press, 1988), 7.

[3]George Barna, *Evangelism That Works* (Nashville: Regal Books, 1995), 117.

[4]Merriam-Webster, Inc., *Merriam-Webster's Desk Dictionary* (Springfield, MA: Merriam-Webster, Inc., 1995), 188.

[5]David Kitchens, Luther Rice University. Lithonia, GA, 2006.

[6]Merriam-Webster, Inc, *Merriam-Webster's Desk Dictionary* (Springfield, MA: Merriam-Webster, Inc., 1995), 157.

[7]R.J. Rummel, *The Statistics of Democide: Genocide and Mass Murder Since 1900* (Charlottesville, VA: Rutgers University Publishers, 1997).

[8]Ibid.
[9]George Barna, *Evangelism That Works* (Nashville: Regal Books, 1995), 23.

[10]Jerry Vines and Jim Shaddix, *Power in the Pulpit* (Chicago: Moody Press, 1999), 13.
[11]Dean Finley, *Handbook for Youth Evangelism* (Nashville: Broadman Press, 1988), 7.

[12]Wesley Black, Chap Clark, and Melan Nel, *Four Views of Youth Ministry and the Church* (Grand Rapids, MI: Zondervan Publishing House, 2001).

Chapter Four

[1]Norman Geisler and Peter Bocchino, *Unshakable Foundations.* (Bloomington, MN: Bethany House Publishers, 2001), 55.

[2]Merriam-Webster, Inc., *Merriam-Webster's Desk Dictionary,* Springfield, MA: Merriam-Webster, Inc., (1995).

[3]Derek L. Phillips. "Relativism, Morality, and Feminist Thought." *Cognitive Relativism & Social Science* (1992): 227-241.

[4]David P. Gushee. "Our Missing Moral Compass." *Christianity Today* 49 (2005): 88.

[5]Charles M.A. Clark. "Christian Morals and the Competitive System Revisited." *Journal of Economic Issues* (2006): 260.

[6]Gerald Skool. "The Nature of Science and the Study of Biological Evolution." *Journal of College Science Teaching* 4 (2006): 74-75.

[7]Norman Geisler and Peter Bocchino, *Unshakable Foundations*. (Bloomington, MN: Bethany House Publishers, 2001), 141.
[8]Ibid., 115.

[9]Ibid., 170.

[10]Charles Darwin, *The Origin of Species*. London: John Murray, 1859.

[11]Ibid., 170.

[12]Norman Geisler and Peter Bocchino, *Unshakable Foundations*. (Bloomington, MN: Bethany House Publishers, 2001), 94.

[13]Ibid., 206.

[14]Ibid., 206.

[15]Ibid., 14.

Chapter Five

[1]Ted Slater. "1% Myth", 2007. http://www.boundless.org.

[2]Merriam-Webster, Inc., *Merriam-Webster's Desk Dictionary*, Springfield, MA: Merriam-Webster, Inc., (1995).

[3]Stephen Jay Gould. "Abscheulich (Atrocious!): Haeckel's distortions did not help Darwin." *Journal of Natural History* (2000): March.

[4]John G. West and Casey Luskin, "Hoax of Dodos." Discovery Institute (2007).

[5]Ibid.

[6]Norman Geisler and Peter Bocchino, *Unshakable Foundations*. Bloomington, MN: Bethany House Publishers, 2001.

[7]Ibid.

[8]Charles Darwin, *The Origin of Species*. London: John Murray, 1859.

[9]http://www.veritas-ucsb.org/library/origins/quotes/Discontinuties.html, 2008.

[10]David Raup, "Conflicts Between Darwin and Paleontology." *Field Museum of Natural History Bulletin* (1979): 50.

[11]Norman Geisler and Peter Bocchino, *Unshakable Foundations*. Bloomington, MN: Bethany House Publishers, 2001.
[12]R.Monastersky. "Smuggled Chinese dinosaur to fly home." *Science News* (1999): 156.

[13]John MacArthur, *A Battle for the Beginning: Creation, Evolution, and the Bible*. Nashville: Nelson Publishing, 2001, 98.

[14]Ibid.

[15]"War Against the Weak: Eugenics and America's Campaign to Create a Master Race." *The Washington Post* (2003): T.10.

[16]Ibid

Chapter Six

[1]"Plato's Shorter Ethical Works", July 6, 2005. http://plato.stanford.edu/entries/plato-ethics-shorter/ (27 May Feb 2008)

[3]*Funk and Wagner's Standard College Dictionary*, managing ed. Sidney i. Landau, s.v. "common" (New York: Harcourt, Brace and World Inc., 1966), p. 273.

[3]Ibid., 749.

[4]David J. Murray, *A History of Western Psychology* (Englewood Cliffs, NJ: Prentice Hall, Inc., 1988), 417.

[5]"Psychology, Counseling and Selfism", http://www.creationism.org/csshs/v12n1p26.htm (18June 2008).

[6]Thomas Hardy Leahy, *A History of Psychology: Main Currents in Psychological Thought* (Englewood Cliffs, NJ: Prentice Hall, Inc., 1987), 433

[7]Ibid., 433-434.

[8]Ibid., 435.

[9]Jay E. Adams, *The Christian Counselor's Manual* (Grand Rapids, MI: Zondervan Publishing House, 1973), 84.

[10]Ibid., 84-85.

[11]Neil T. Anderson, Terry E. Zuehlke, and Julianne S. Zuehlke, *Christ Centered Therapy: The Practical Integration of Theology and Psychology* (Grand Rapids, MI: Zondervan Publishing House, 2000), 30.

[12]Jay E. Adams, *The Christian Counselor's Manual* (Grand Rapids, MI: Zondervan Publishing House, 1973), 85.

[13]Ibid., 74.

[14]"Plato's Shorter Ethical Works", July 6, 2005. http://plato.stanford.edu/entries/plato-ethics-shorter/ (27 May Feb 2008)

[15]*Funk and Wagner's Standard College Dictionary*, managing ed. Sidney i. Landau, s.v. "expert, knowledge," (New York: Harcourt, Brace and World Inc., 1966), p. 468.

[16]Ibid., 749.

[17]James A. Schellenberg, *Masters of Social Psychology* (New York: Oxford University Press), 1978, 36.

[18]Peter D. Kramer, *Freud Inventor of the Modern Mind* (New York: Harper Collins Publishers, 2006).

[19]Paul C. Vitz, *Sigmund Freud's Christian Unconscious* (New York: The Gilford Press, 1988), 110-111.

[20]Peter Gay, *Freud A Life for Our Time* (New York: W.W. Norton and Company, 1998), 69.

[21]*Funk and Wagner's Standard College Dictionary*, managing ed. Sidney i. Landau, s.v. "expert, knowledge," (New York: Harcourt, Brace and World Inc., 1966), p. 468.

[22]B.F. Skinner, *Reflections on Behaviorism and Society* (Englewood Cliffs, N.J.: Prentice-Hall Inc., 1978), 225.

[23]James A. Schellenberg, *Masters of Social Psychology* (New York: Oxford University Press), 1978, 112.

[24]B.F. Skinner, *Reflections on Behaviorism and Society* (Englewood Cliffs, N.J: Prentice-Hall, Inc., 1978), 125.

[25]Jay E. Adams, *The Christian Counselor's Manual* (Grand Rapids, MI: Zondervan Publishing House, 1973), 73.

[26]Ibid., 74.

[27]Millard J. Erickson, *Christian Theology* (Grand Rapids, MI: Baker Academic, 1998), 715.

[28]Ronald Cobb. Class Lecture Notes, The Active Counseling Stage, Part 1. Luther Rice University, Spring, 2007.

[29]Jeffrey S. Siker, *Homosexuality in the Church*. Louisville: Westminster John Knox Press. 1994.

[30]American Psychological Association. "Answers to Your Questions About Sexual Orientation and Homosexuality", 2007. http://www.apa.org/topics/orientation.html.

Chapter Seven

[1]Jay E. Adams, *The Christian Counselor's Manual* (Grand Rapids, MI: Zondervan Publishing House, 1973), 52.

[2]Ibid., 54-55.

[3]Ibid., 55.

[4]Ibid., 55.

[5]Ibid., 55.

[6]Ibid., 56 .

[7]Earl & Sandy Wilson, Paul & Virginia Frieson, and Larry & Nancy Paulson. *Restoring the Fallen: A Team Approach to Caring, Confronting & Reconciling* (Downer's Grove, IL: InterVarsity Press, 1997), 126.

[8]Ibid, 127.

[9]Ibid, 127.

[10]Ibid, 128.

[11]Ibid, 129-130

[12]Ed Glasscock, Luther Rice University. Lithonia, GA, 2007.

[13]Ibid.
[14]Ibid.

[15]Merriam-Webster, Inc. *Merriam-Webster's Desk Dictionary* (Springfield, MA: Merriam-Webster, Inc., 1995).
[16]The Holy Bible; King James Version. Uhrichsville, OH: Barbour Publishing, 2002.

[17]Robert Jamison, A.R. Fausset, David, Brown, *Commentary Critical and Explanatory on the Whole Bible* (Bellingham, WA: Logos Research Systems, Inc, 1997).

[18]Matthew Henry, *Matthew Henry's Concise Commentary on the Whole Bible* (Nashville: Thomas Nelson Inc., 1997).

[19]Jim Kinnebrew. Class Lecture Notes, "I am a Success." Luther Rice University, Fall, 2007.

[20]Kenneth Boa. *Conformed to His Image* (Grand Rapids, MI: Zondervan, 2001), 180.

[21]Donald S. Whitney. *Spiritual Disciplines for the Christian life* (Colorado Springs: NavPress, 1991), 77.

[22]Donald S. Whitney. *Spiritual Disciplines for the Christian life* (Colorado Springs: NavPress, 1991), 77.

GLOSSARY

A

Academia: Pertaining to a school or place of instruction

Adolescent: Phase in a person's life which lies between childhood and adulthood; considered by experts to be ages ten to eighteen

Agnostic: A person who holds the view that any ultimate reality (as God) is unknown and probably unknowable

Apartheid: Racial segregation; a former policy of segregation and political and economic discrimination against non-European groups in the Republic of South Africa

Apologetics: defense of the divine origin and authority of Christianity

Argument: a reason given in proof or rebuttal

Atheist: one who believes there is no deity (God)

B

Behaviorism: A school of psychology that takes the objective evidence of behavior as the only concern of its research and the only basis of its theory without reference to conscious experience

C

Cell: The smallest structural unit of living matter capable of functioning independently

cf.: Reference

Clarity: To make something clear

Common Knowledge: An acquaintance or understanding held by a community as a truth

Condemn/Condemnation: To declare to be reprehensible, wrong, or evil usually after weighing evidence and without reservation; to pronounce guilty

Contradiction: A proposition, statement, or phrase that asserts or implies both the truth and falsity of something

Creationism: The understanding that God created everything, versus it just happening on its own

D

Darwinism: A theory that all of life began from one cell; then evolved to the different life forms and still evolves, and that forces in nature only allow the best to continue to evolve

Democide: The murder of any person or people by a government

Deism: System of thought advocating natural religion, emphasizing morality, and denying the interference of the Creator with the laws of the universe.

Detrimental: obviously harmful; damaging

Diligent: Characterized by steady, earnest, and energetic effort

Disciple: One who accepts and assists in spreading the doctrines of another

Doctrine: Something that is taught; a body of principles or system of belief

Dogmatic: Characterized by or given to the expression of opinions very strongly or positively as if they were facts

E

e.g.: For example

Embryo: A vertebrate at any stage of development prior to birth or hatching.

Embryonic Recapitulation: A theory that claims the embryos of several different animals and that of a human appear to be almost identical at the first stage of their lives

Emeritus: One who has retired from a position, but are still actively involved in the duties that position requires

Entropy: Systems in nature tend to move toward disorder as energy is dispersed; things wear out as time goes by

Epistemologically Inferior Logical Operation: Not having the ability to replace bad moral values with good moral values; immature in one's level of morality

Epistemologically Superior Logical Operation: The ability to replace bad moral values with good moral values; mature in one's level of morality

Evangelism: The winning or revival of personal commitments to Christ

Evolution: A theory that animals and plants have gradually changed over the years from simpler forms of life to become what they are today

Ex Nihilo: Latin for—out of nothing

Exegesis: An explanation or critical interpretation of a text

Expert Knowledge: Teachable, learnable techniques held by formally trained persons, which non-trained persons can rely upon for help

F

Faith: Belief and trust in and loyalty to God

Feminism: The theory of the political, economic, and social equality of the sexes

First Principle of Logic: The understanding that one doesn't start with a theory and work their way back to the truth. They start, rather, with the truth to work out any theories

Fossil: A remnant [remains] of an organism from a past geological age, such as an animal skeleton or leaf imprint which is embedded and preserved in the earth's crust

Freudianism: Psychology or philosophy that follows the psychoanalytic theories or practices of Sigmund Freud

G

Gap theory: A theory that claims there is an undetermined amount of time between the verses of Genesis 1:1 and 1:2 allowing for the possibility of evolution

Genealogies: Family tree or ancestry

Genocide: The deliberate and systematic destruction of a racial, political, or cultural group

Glory: A distinguished quality or asset

Gnostic: A belief that certain knowledge is only held by a small elite group

Gospel: The message concerning Christ, the kingdom of God, and salvation

Great Commission, The: A special calling from Jesus Christ to His followers to teach, baptize and make disciples throughout the earth in the name of the Father, Son, and Holy Spirit

Gradualism: Evolution through gradual changes in species over long periods of time

H

Hermeneutics: The study of the methodological principles of interpretation (as of the Bible)

Holy Spirit: The third person of the Christian trinity; the Holy Ghost; Spirit

Humanism: A belief that usually rejects supernaturalism (God) and stresses an individual's dignity and worth and capacity for self-realization through reasoning

Hypotheses: an assumption or concession made for the sake of argument

I

i.e.: That is

Imago Dei: Latin for Image of God

Implode: To collapse or fail without external assistance; to break down or fall apart from within

Inherit: To receive from a parent or ancestor by genetic transmission

Intellectual Honesty: The idea that anything is debatable

L

Law of Non Contradiction: An understanding that it is not possible for something to be both true and not true at the same time and in the same context

M

Mass Murder: Murdering a large number of people, typically at the same time or over a relatively short period of time

Maturation Process: Act of becoming mature (older and perhaps wiser or better developed)

Misnomer: A wrong name or inappropriate designation

Missing Link: a hypothetical form of animal assumed to have constituted a connecting link between the anthropoid apes and humans

Morality: The conformity to ideals of right human conduct.

N

Natural Selection: The idea that only the best genetic qualities of a species survive in nature.

Naturalism: A theory denying that an event or object has a supernatural significance (i.e. nothing outside of nature, including God, has anything to do with what happens.)

Nazism: The body of political and economic beliefs Nazis in Germany held and carried out from 1933 to 1945 which stated the government should have complete control of people and that Germanic groups were racially superior to all others.

Nouthetic Counseling: Biblical counseling based on instruction, correction or encouragement.

O

Objective: Expressing or dealing with facts or conditions as perceived without distortion by personal feelings, prejudices, or interpretations

One Percent Myth: A false belief that humans and chimps have 99 percent of their DNA in common

P

Paleontology: The study of life forms existing in prehistoric times as represented by fossil remains of plants, animals, and other organisms

Panentheism: A belief that God's physical body is the universe and everything in it; very similar to Pantheism. It is also a belief in a genderless God

Pantheism: The worship of all gods of different creeds, cults, or peoples indifferently or equates God with the forces and laws of the universe

Passage: A usually brief portion of a written work

Philosophy: The most basic beliefs, concepts, and attitudes of an individual or group

Politicide: The deliberate and systematic destruction of a racial, political, or cultural group strictly for political reasons

Potential: Capable of development into actuality

Presupposition: A belief based on prior information; an assumption

Principle: A comprehensive and fundamental law, doctrine, or assumption

Protestant: A Christian not of a Catholic or Eastern Church

Psychoanalysis: A method of psychology which treats emotional disorders in sessions where the patient is encouraged to talk freely about personal experiences and especially about early childhood and dreams

R

Radiocarbon Dating: The determination of the approximate age of an ancient object, such as an archaeological specimen, by measuring the amount of carbon 14 it contains. Also called carbon dating.

Reconcile: To restore to friendship or harmony

Reconciliation/Discipline Dynamic: The idea that God disciplines people in an attempt to establish the proper relationship between He and them

Redeem: To free from whatever distresses or harms; to buy back.

Refute: To prove wrong

Relativism: A theory that knowledge is relative to the limited nature of the mind and the conditions of knowing; a view that ethical truths depend on the individuals and groups holding them

Religion: A cause, principle, or system of beliefs held to with ardor and faith

Repentance: To turn from sin and dedicate oneself to the amendment of one's life

Resurrection: The state of one risen from the dead

Rogerianism: A belief that each person has the power within themselves to obtain healing of psychological problems via knowledge which is common to all

Romans Road: Passages of Scripture within the book of Romans that identify God's plan of salvation for humankind

S

Salvation: Deliverance from the power and effects of sin

Saved: Having obtained salvation

Savior: One who saves from danger or destruction; one who brings salvation

Scholar: A person who has done advanced study in a special field

Scientific Proof: Verified or verifiable information

Scientific Law: a statement that explains what something does in science, which is confirmed and broadly agreed upon

Second Law of Thermodynamics: Based on scientific study, has noted how the universe is in a state of increasing entropy. Substance in nature has a tendency to wear down, rather than improve.

Secular: Of or relating to worldly or temporal

Self-discipline: Correction or regulation of oneself for the sake of improvement

Seminary: An institution for the training of candidates for the priesthood, ministry, or rabbinate

Sic: Quoted directly from the source using original spelling and context even if they are incorrect

Systematic: Reduced complexity, streamlined, methodical steps taken to come to the concluded facts found in study

Systematic Adolescent Theology: The non-complex steps one can take to prepare others (specifically youth and young adults) with what one has studied and know about God

Sin: Transgression of the law of God; a defective state of human nature in which the self is estranged from God

Spirit: A supernatural being or essence; when capitalized, the Holy Spirit.

Spiritual Discipline: Correction or regulation of oneself for the sake of improving a relationship with God

Spirituality: Sensitivity or attachment to Christian values

Subjectivity: Modified or affected by personal views, experience, or background

T

Text: The original words and form of a written or printed work

Theologian: Those who spend many years studying and knowing God's Word

Theology: The study and knowledge of God

Theory: An unproven assumption

Trinity: The unity of Father, Son, and Holy Spirit as three persons in one Godhead

Triune: See Trinity

V

Vessel: A person into whom some quality (as grace) is infused

W

Worldview: A person's perception of all reality based on the things they see, know and believe

INDEX

ABOUT THE AUTHOR

James Gamble is married to Lucinda (1986) and they have two college kids: James, II and Marcinda. He is currently the Youth Pastor at Big Miller Grove Missionary Baptist Church in Lithonia (Atlanta), GA. James has also authored *Exposed!*. Outside of ministry, his interests include family, sports, fishing, motorcycles and his old '63 Chevy truck. He holds a Ph.D. in Psychology with a concentration in Christian Counseling from Louisiana Baptist University in Shreveport, Louisiana. He is a member of the American Association of Christian Counselors.